Contexts in Literature

The Gothic Tradition

David Stevens

Series editor: Adrian Barlow

CAMBRIDGE
UNIVERSITY PRESS

CAMBRIDGE
UNIVERSITY PRESS

University Printing House, Cambridge CB2 8BS, United Kingdom

Cambridge University Press is part of the University of Cambridge.

It furthers the University's mission by disseminating knowledge in the pursuit of education, learning and research at the highest international levels of excellence.

www.cambridge.org
Information on this title: www.cambridge.org/9780521777322

© Cambridge University Press 2000

First published 2000
15th printing 2013

Printed in the United Kingdom by Printondemand-worldwide, Peterborough

A catalogue record for this publication is available from the British Library

Acknowledgements

The author and publishers wish to thank the following for permission to use copyright material:

Sheil Land Associates Ltd on behalf of the author for an extract from Susan Hill *The Woman in Black*, Vintage, pp 94–96, plus a short extract from the Introduction, Longman edition. Copyright © Susan Hill 1983; and short extracts from Susan Hill *I'm the King of the Castle*, Vintage. Copyright © Susan Hill 1970, and the Afterword, Penguin edition (1989).
Every effort has been made to reach copyright holders; the publishers would like to hear from anyone whose rights they have unknowingly infringed.

Thanks are also due to AKG London for permission to reproduce the photograph on page 11.

ISBN 978-0-521-77732-2 Paperback

Prepared for publication by Gill Stacey
Designed by Tattersall Hammarling & Silk
Cover photo: © *Bob Krist/Corbis (detail)*

Contents

Introduction

To look for 'gothic' websites on the Internet is to come up with a bewildering range of possibilities. At various points in the long and ever-growing list of mainly American 'gothic' sites, often dedicated to selling products such as music and fashion icons, there may be more academic areas featuring historical, political, literary and musical associations – to name but a few. Such is the eclecticism of the gothic world that the label has been and is applied to virtually every aspect of human creativity. It is partly this wide range of characteristics which makes the gothic both attractive and confusing. Part of the function of this book is to offer some guidance: not in terms of a fixed or definitive set of characteristics, but rather in giving a framework for questions and explorations. The focus throughout tends to be on the Western European cultural world of the latter half of the 18th century and the beginning of the 19th, as befits English literary study, but the context is far broader. The gothic influence on such modern writers as Angela Carter, Iain Banks or Stephen King, for instance, is vivid and great as is the effect on the worlds of film and rock music. If the context is broad, so too is the appeal, both during past times and today, and this helps to explain the huge number of possible 'gothic' websites, publications and other resources to choose from.

It would be contrary to the spirit of the gothic to attempt to pin it down too absolutely or to limit it to narrow explanation. Nevertheless, if too loose a conception of the gothic is used, applied vaguely and without differentiation to virtually every form of human activity, it must inevitably lose something of its cutting edge. It is precisely the tension between these approaches – the one inclusive and eclectic, the other seeking a sharp focus and clarity of definition – that characterises the explorations encountered in this book.

Critics and commentators have ventured many and often conflicting opinions on the nature of the gothic, never more so than today, when there has been an alarming – and perhaps intimidating – diversification of critical opinion. Here again there are tensions and oppositions, but also the possibilities of creative cross-fertilisation. One of the main aims of this book is to help the reader achieve some degree of critical synthesis – combining aspects of various views to create a coherent appraisal – through seeing gothic texts in context. Consider, for example, these views of the gothic phenomenon:

> … this recurrent pattern of primitive thinking, appearing from the period from about 1760 to 1830, is symptomatic of the sudden dislocation, challenge to, or loss of faith in the theological interpretation of nature before there was a scientific one to replace it.
> (from Marilyn Gaull *English Romanticism: The Human Context*, 1988)

[*The Castle of*] *Otranto* [Horace Walpole's pioneering gothic novel of 1764] looks uncommonly like an attempt to graft on to the novel – that modern form concerned with money, possessions, status, circumstance – the heightened passions, elemental situations, and stylised poetic techniques of the Elizabethan dramatists.

(from Marilyn Butler *Romantics, Rebels and Reactionaries*, 1981)

The continuum that links the gothic to the 'domestic novel' is marked by the fact that however arcane or historic the setting, it is always linked to the desire of contemporary readers. At once escapist and conformist, the gothic speaks to the dark side of domestic fiction: erotic, violent, perverse, bizarre and occasionally connected with contemporary fears.

(from *Gothic Horror*, ed Clive Bloom, 1998)

It is worth asking whether these views complement or conflict with each other, and with some of the other interpretations and opinions put forward. Only through rigorous examination may some sort of critical synthesis be arrived at. The three writers quoted above are just some of the commentators and critics whose opinions will be encountered and investigated in this book. There is a common purpose here: to see the gothic (in particular, gothic literature) in context – or rather, in a series of contexts, including diverse and often challenging critical contexts. To understand the gothic, it is vital to connect with it in its broadest sense: with the contemporary historical and cultural contexts; with the variety of art forms; with critical opinion; with the modern age, and its own concerns and obsessions. The extracts and whole short texts included in this book are intended to give a flavour of gothic writing, a tasting session which may be followed up by a more comprehensive exploration of some of the key texts, including those listed on pages 121–124. Contextual and critical investigations are certainly important, but gothic texts are intended to be enjoyed above all else. It is in this spirit that this book has been written.

How the book is organised

Part 1: Approaching the gothic tradition
Part 1 is a survey of the gothic tradition, particularly as seen through its literature. It examines the historical and cultural contexts of the gothic at its height in the 18th and 19th centuries, and the place of the gothic in today's world.

Part 2: Approaching the texts
Part 2 considers the different elements that make literary texts 'gothic', and relates these to a wide range of gothic texts.

Part 3: Texts and extracts
Part 3 contains texts and extracts to illustrate key themes and points in the rest of the book, or to suggest a focus for tasks and assignments.

Part 4: Critical approaches
This part explores the different ways in which critics and readers have reacted to gothic literature.

Part 5: How to write about the gothic
Part 5 offers guidelines and assignments for those for whom this book is chiefly intended: students covering the topic as part of an advanced course in literary studies.

Part 6: Resources
This part contains a chronology of texts and writers discussed in the book, together with guidance on further reading, and a glossary and index. (Terms which appear in the glossary are highlighted in bold type when they first appear in the main text.)

At different points throughout the book, and at the end of Parts 1, 2, 4 and 5, there are tasks and assignments which suggest a variety of contexts through which students might approach an understanding of particular works.

1 | Approaching the gothic tradition

- What are the significant social, political and cultural events and developments of the period from approximately 1750 to 1820?

- What historical information may be useful in developing a thorough understanding of literature, particularly gothic texts, written during the period?

- What does the term 'gothic' mean in its historical sense?

- What is the place of the gothic in today's world?

The term 'gothic' commands a vast semantic field of varied terrain: a range of possible meanings, definitions and associations. It explicitly denotes certain historical and cultural phenomena - in many respects the primary foci of this book – but the connotations and associations are far broader. The chronology on pages 120–121 aims to provide a skeletal outline of key texts and writers; this part will elaborate on the detail and some of the subtleties involved – assembling the parts and attempting to breathe life into the whole.

The historical context

Historically, the Goths were one of several Germanic tribes instrumental in the disintegration of the Roman Empire in the 4th century. In the following centuries historians came to regard the Goths almost generically as all Germans – including, of course, the Anglo-Saxons who settled in the British Isles. From this position, subsequent historians and propagandists were able to proclaim a 'native' freedom-loving gothic tradition within British culture, in opposition to 'foreign' imperialism as epitomised by the Norman invasion of 1066 and the authoritarian rule it ushered in. This was powerful myth making, and its essential elements may be clearly seen in popular legends such as that of Robin Hood, celebrating righteous Anglo-Saxon rebellion against the Norman tyrannical yoke.

By the 18th century, when agitation for political and social reform was gathering momentum, this interpretation of history had a ready and enthusiastic following amongst those who saw authoritarian monarchy, with all its attendant institutions, rules and conventions, as increasingly anachronistic. To celebrate the original gothic love of liberty was in effect to argue for greater contemporary freedom through political reform: the reformist wing of the **Whig Party**, in particular, embraced such ideals in opposition to **Tory** ideology. James Thomson, for example, in his appropriately titled long poem 'Liberty' (1735–1736), celebrated the original Goths:

```
                                    ... untamed
To the refining subtleties of slaves,
They brought a happy government along;
Formed by that freedom which, with secret voice,
Impartial nature teaches all her sons.
```
                                                    (iv 680–684)

Despite this over-simplifying of such history – or perhaps precisely because of it –
these ideas found fertile ground in the political landscape of the 18th century and
helped to foster the rise of the gothic. At the same time, however, there is evidence
to suggest that those on the right of the political spectrum, broadly represented by
the Tory Party, also made use of the 'gothic' label for their own political ends. In
this interpretation of British history, the gothic represented tradition, hierarchy
and aristocracy as against dangerous modern, democratic – or at least populist –
ideas. As the critic Victor Sage maintains, '... the term "Gothick" itself is an
ambiguous one, incorporating many shades and combinations of association. For
the 18th century reader, it was an almost unpredictable intersection of religious
belief, of aesthetic taste and political inclination.' (from *The Gothick Novel: A
Selection of Critical Essays*, ed. Victor Sage, 1990)

History as narrative rather than science enabled its interpreters to merge times
and places without too much concern for accuracy. By the time the term 'gothic'
(or 'gothick', as it was more frequently spelled) became fairly common currency in
the mid-18th century there had occurred a certain elision of historical epochs, so
that gothic seems to have referred to the medieval rather than to the pre-Norman
conquest epoch. Thus the text generally taken to be the first – and in many ways
archetypal – gothic novel, Horace Walpole's *The Castle of Otranto* (1764), was
subtitled *A Gothic Story* to hint at the period in which it was set: the medieval.
Indeed, Walpole initially concocted an elaborate deceit that the novel was written by
an Italian canon, Onuphrio Muralto, some time between the 11th and 13th
centuries. The reader must beware here, as always, of trying to put too explicit a fix
on the gothic, however. In effect, as with most linguistic developments, including
those today, the term may refer to a host of sometimes complementary, sometimes
contradictory ideas.

There are so many gothic associations that the whole concept may seem at
times indefinable and elusive. Nevertheless, emerging from this rather uneven,
often misleading semantic field is a sense of the gothic as recovering and renewing
a tradition which valued feelings and sensibility, and which had been all but
usurped by the developing dominance of reason as the key to all human problems.
Reason and rationality had achieved this pre-eminence as fundamental
philosophical characteristics of the historical phenomenon known as the

Enlightenment, itself a reaction against superstition and blind adherence to tradition in favour of scientific, open enquiry. The 18th century was in many ways the high point of the Enlightenment, especially in Britain. In historical terms the medieval period pre-dated the Enlightenment, just as in terms of the growth of each individual person the emotions come before and can therefore be seen as more profoundly human than the insistence on rationality. At the same time, social progress, relying largely on more and more rationally based political and social organisation and on various scientific and technological inventions, had made it comparatively 'safe' to indulge in irrational fantasies. Middle class readers, safely tucked into their stable and unthreatened social positions, could feel secure enough to cultivate imaginary fears and fantasies, in the same way that a child may do, reading horror stories and experiencing the delicious thrill while apparently immune from real danger. This is perhaps to belittle the impact of the emerging gothic, however, for the general trend towards an aesthetic more fully in touch with feeling and emotion was profound and real. Widespread awareness that over-reliance on reason could rob human experience of its essential flavour was increasingly characteristic of the age.

Gothic influences

Many of the early manifestations of what came to be called the gothic were not in the area of literature at all, but in art, in architecture, and in landscape gardening. These art forms provide the contexts for literature; they are also, clearly, more public and generally more expensive in their manifestations. As such, they tended, in the 18th century, to be largely the preserve of the aristocracy. Reading, on the other hand, with widening literacy, was more open to the up-and-coming middle classes, including – particularly for the novel – women.

Art in opposition: Goya and Blake

Emerging from all these connotations and shifts in meaning is a clear sense of the gothic in opposition to neo-classical notions of 'good order' and 'good taste' which were founded on a fundamental belief in rationalism. These neo-classical ideas had emerged as the dominant aesthetic – or sense of what is beautiful and artistically valid – of the later 17th and earlier 18th centuries. As the gothic clearly relates to all art forms, it may be fitting to begin a more detailed examination of the phenomenon in its historical context not with literature, but with a picture: 'The Sleep of Reason Produces Monsters', drawn by the Spanish artist Goya (1746–1828) in 1799. (This picture appears opposite.) It is one of a series of prints, and has been called 'perhaps the most important single image for the historian of the gothic' (from *Gothic: Four Hundred Years of Excess, Horror, Evil and Ruin*, 1998). It depicts a sleeping man slumped at a desk, his face hidden by his arms in a

'El sueño de la razon produce monstruos'

posture suggesting desperation. The pen and paper on the desk seem to indicate that he is a writer. Strange blood-sucking bats hover above, receding into the surrounding darkness; they seem both to emanate from and horribly threaten the prostrate figure. The very title of Goya's picture signals the gothic message: when reason sleeps, as everything must, the hitherto repressed monsters will emerge, both threatening and terrifying precisely because they have been repressed.

Goya's own manuscript notes on a trial proof clarify the message succinctly: 'Fantasy abandoned by reason produces impossible monsters; united with it, she is the mother of the arts and origin of its marvels.' As such, this message prefigures Sigmund Freud's (1856–1939) later insights into psychological repression and its potentially devastating impact on mental health (see pages 102–104). It also finds an echo in the writing of Goya's contemporary William Blake (1757–1827), much of whose poetry deals with the realisation that to repress emotions and feelings is to make them all the more terrifyingly distorted when they do, inevitably, emerge. For Blake, writing in his appropriately titled *The Marriage of Heaven and Hell* (1793), the angels represent reliance purely on reason, whereas the poet or artist has the duty to uncover the world of the imagination. Thus, '... I was walking among the fires of Hell, delighted with the enjoyments of genius, which to angels look like torment and insanity'. Goya, 'the greatest painter to have had gothic moods' (Davenport-Hines), and the goths also walked among the fires of hell, apparently delighting in the enjoyments of genius. And, as may be seen at various points in this book, more conventional citizens ('angels'?) certainly tended to see only torment and insanity.

▶ Examine as many as possible of works of art which have gothic associations, noting common themes and subjects. As you study more gothic texts, including those featured in this book, try to relate these pictures to the written word. What might the pictorial arts offer in this context that writing might find more difficult to convey?

As well as Goya's 'Sleep of Reason', you may like to consider the following pictures, or other examples by these artists:

- 'The Nightmare' (1782) by Henry Fuseli (1745–1846)

- 'Chatterton receiving Poison from the Spirit of Despair' (1780) by John Flaxman (1755–1826)

- 'Good and Evil Angels' (1795) by William Blake

- 'The Cross in the Mountains' (1808) by Caspar David Friedrich (1774–1840)

- 'The Bard' (1817) by John Martin (1789–1854)

- 'The Death of Sardanapalus' (1827) by Eugene Delacroix (1798–1863)

- 'The Fairy-Feller's Master Stroke' (1864) by Richard Dadd (1817–1886)
- illustrations to Coleridge's 'The Rime of the Ancient Mariner', particularly 'Death and Life-in-Death dicing for the soul of the Mariner' (1875) by Gustav Doré (1832–1883).

Other art forms: gothic buildings and 'landscapes'

Throughout the 18th century, wealthy aristocratic patrons commissioned a series of ever more extravagant gothic buildings and 'landscapes', a trend that would continue well into the 19th century and even beyond. William Kent (1686–1748), an artist, architect and landscape designer, was hired by many wealthy patrons to transform their habitats, and achieved celebrity status. Interestingly, several of the major gothic writers, notably Horace Walpole and William Beckford, also had the enthusiasm and money to have gothic edifices built – at Strawberry Hill and Fonthill Abbey respectively. Kent's ideas, themselves largely borrowed from continental sources, became the inspiration for a generation of designers and their employers, vying with each other to achieve ever more sensational effects. Mock abbeys, castles and hunting lodges (all suitably 'ruined') became increasingly widespread. Kent even went so far as to suggest 'planting' dead trees in order to present an appropriately ghoulish effect. Gothic design was even to become the dominant aesthetic force in Britain – the building symbolic of the very essence of the establishment, the Houses of Parliament, was based on the detailed design drawings of Augustus Pugin (1812–1852). Not all gothic-inspired buildings had similar staying power, however. Beckford's exotic creation Fonthill Abbey, designed by James Wyatt (1746–1813), suffered the collapse of its first grandiose 300 foot tower in 1800, followed by its replacement structure twenty five years later, after Beckford had sold the property. It subsequently fell into complete, genuine (as opposed to feigned) ruin. In a sense this was a fitting gothic culmination of the whole project, and the impression from Beckford's own observations is that it was the process rather than the final product which mattered to him. His description of the building work, in 1808, is itself evocative gothic prose:

> ... it's really stupendous, the spectacle here at night ... the innumerable torches suspended everywhere, the immense and endless spaces, the gulph below; above, the gigantic spider's web of scaffolding ... immense buckets of plaster and water ascending, as if they were drawn up from the bowels of a mine, amid shouts from subterranean depths, oaths from Hell itself, and chanting from Pandemonium ...'

After such excitement, what satisfaction could there possibly be in simply living in the place?

These very concrete manifestations of the gothic – buildings, pictures, man-made landscapes – perhaps suggest that it was primarily concerned with visible creations rather than the subtleties of inner thoughts and feelings. The critic Emma McEvoy, for example, in her introduction to Lewis's *The Monk*, has noted the fairly widely held view that the 'Gothic is a kind of pre-Romanticism that enacts a literalisation of the Romantic metaphor'. Whereas **Romanticism** proper is held to deal with the subtleties of human feelings and visions in various artistic expressions – mountains, rivers, dreams, for example – the gothic, according to this view, attempted to make these metaphorical insights real and actual. Real 'castles' were indeed built, and whole landscapes changed. In so doing, clearly, much of the metaphorical meaning was in danger of being lost. So the gothic may be seen with hindsight as a rather clumsy, externally orientated transition phase in the progress towards mature Romanticism. There may be something in this, and in the end each student of the gothic has to judge on the available evidence.

▶ Explore any gothic architectural or landscape garden examples in your own locality, using whatever resources are readily available. Genuine gothic architecture of the medieval period is likely to be limited to cathedrals, churches and abbeys, often featuring such characteristics as gothic arches over windows and doors, flying buttresses, impressive towers, castellated walls, and macabre gargoyles. Some acquaintance with these buildings should help to give a clearer idea of the inspiration for the 'gothic revival' of the 18th and 19th centuries. Examples from these later times may need some discovering: 'follies' (mock towers, hunting lodges and the like) on large estates, often now owned by the National Trust or English Heritage, are certainly fascinating indicators of gothic taste. The National Trust and the local Tourist Information Office should be able to provide information on possible locations.

Poetry

Certainly the gothic was a great borrower of diverse ideas from eclectic sources, many of which will be mentioned in the context of closer textual study in Parts 2 and 3. Spenser, Shakespeare, Milton, German 'Schauer-Romantic' ('horror-romantic') literature, folk tales and ballads, and popular superstitions all found their way into the gothic idiom. One direct precursor of and influence on the gothic, for instance, was the 18th century 'Graveyard' school of poetry: typically, melancholy poems dwelling on the theme of death in a graveyard setting. 'Night Thoughts' (1742), written by Edward Young (1683–1765) and subsequently illustrated by William Blake, contains these lines:

Silence and Darkness! Solemn sisters! Twins
From ancient night ...
Assist me: I will thank you in the grave –
The grave, your kingdom: there this frame shall fall
A victim sacred to your dreary shrine:
But what are ye?

Robert Blair's 'The Grave' (1743) contains an even more explicit invocation to death, which helped to make it one of the most popular poems of its day:

Thrice welcome Death
That after many a painful bleeding Step
Conducts us to our Home, and lands us safe
On the long-wish'd for shore ...

Graveyard poetry both fed upon the contemporary preoccupation with death and encouraged it, instrumental in creating the fertile conditions for the development of the gothic.

However, great care is again needed here: derivative the gothic may be, but it is impossible to find total originality in any artistic movement. Further, the whole concept of originality is a relatively modern phenomenon (largely alien to Shakespeare, for example), and care must be taken lest we judge aspects of the past by present standards. The real question is not so much concerning originality or its lack, but rather in judging how robust, influential, beneficial or purposeful the gothic was to become.

The political context

Inevitably, this book has touched several times on the political background to the rise of the gothic, noting various connotations and paradoxes. The concern here should be not for narrow party politics – although, as previously discussed, the gothic played its part in the contemporary rise of the Whig and Tory political parties – but rather in the broad social and political changes sweeping across Britain and Europe in the 18th and 19th centuries. Gothic reactions to these movements were often crucial in determining what sort of art and literature was produced. The role of the gothic was not limited simply to reacting to events; gothic ideas and feelings were frequently themselves significant influences. The relationship between historical cause and effect is a complex one, perhaps best envisaged as dialectical – simply, dealing with the conflict or harmony between different parts as the method through which the whole develops and changes. In terms of cause and effect, each part may need each other in order that progress is achieved in some sort of synthesis.

The period with which this book is primarily dealing – roughly that between 1750 and 1820 – was notable for the acceleration of change in just about every sphere of human activity. In particular, it would be hard to over-estimate the impact made by the French Revolution of 1789: an international upheaval which sent shock waves around the whole of the western world, and beyond. The implications of the French Revolution still resonate today; then, it was confusion which characterised many people's responses. As Fred Botting has written 'Uncertainties about the nature of power, law, society, family and sexuality dominate Gothic fiction ... linked to wider threats of disintegration manifested most forcefully in political revolution'. (from *Gothic: The New Critical Idiom*, 1996) Another critic, Robert Kiely, maintains that 'gothic fiction was not only about confusion, it was written from confusion'. (from *The Romantic Novel in England*, 1972) Interestingly, there is a striking resemblance between the final years of the 20th century and the 1790s (and in many ways the 1890s too): uncertainty about how to visualise the future, veering from excited optimism to profound despair. Revolutionary politicisation, reactionary nostalgia, and deliberate escapism are all possible reactions, and all are represented in different ways in the gothic. The common sense stoicism – sometimes more resembling defeatism – with which most people greet the prospect of radical change was perhaps less characteristic of the gothic trend.

In Britain the aristocracy certainly had the resources and power to demolish and build, sometimes changing whole landscapes and flattening villages in order to create a more 'gothic' sensation, but in the 18th century an increasingly wealthy middle class was fast catching up. Newly expanding industries and transport systems were the basis of this new-found wealth and prestige, but the British political system changed only very slowly to reflect the shifting balance of power. The calls for reform, even radical reform, came from many quarters, and by no means only from the truly dispossessed in the chaotically growing towns and chronically impoverished countryside. Even while espousing the cause of political reform, middle class ambivalence towards the aristocracy was marked. On the one hand, many looked with awe at the titles and traditions of the landed gentry; on the other hand, rivalry, competition and sheer hard-nosed business acumen ensured aristocratic excess was frequently caricatured and despised. This tension spilled over into the gothic, and in many respects can be seen as the socio-political dimension of the old–new dichotomy already mentioned. A tension also existed in the emerging middle class's relationship with what were then known as the 'labouring classes' – the necessary pool of usually unskilled workers who actually created the new wealth. Any lasting reform in the political system would have to gain a measure of popular support, but there was a great fear amongst those with property that this support might spill into something more seriously revolutionary.

Again, the tension manifests itself in the gothic – often in a certain ambivalence towards the working class (in the form of servants, or, more ominously, 'the mob', for example) among some of its chief proponents.

The representation of revolutionary ideas and emotions and their subsequent containment within a conservative structure is one way of looking at and interpreting the nature of the gothic – at least in terms of its literature (see also Part 4: Critical approaches, pages 95–111). This may seem essentially reactionary, but it is important to realise that key revolutionary thinkers and writers such as Jean-Jacques Rousseau (1712–1778), Thomas Paine (1737–1809), William Godwin (1756–1836), and Mary Wollstonecraft (1759–1797) also had a place in the gothic panoply, even if this was peripheral.

Key thinkers and writers

Although he died before the French Revolution, Rousseau was one of its seminal influences, instrumental in helping to create the philosophical climate for revolutionary ideas to thrive. In his own life he seemed to personify an early version of the Romantic outsider, both at odds with, and seeking energetically to transform, his social context. In *Emile* (1762) and *Confessions* (published posthumously, 1781–1788) Rousseau presented a detailed critique of the relations between society and the individual which found echoes – albeit often distorted ones – in gothic and subsequently Romantic art. He was also vilified as a 'gothic scoundrel'. Edmund Burke (1729–1797), a highly influential conservative philosopher and writer, denounced his 'deranged eccentric vanity', while Ann Radcliffe's gothic novel *The Mysteries of Udolpho* may be read as a refutation of Rousseau's educational ideals: her main character Emily corresponding to his fictional Emile.

Thomas Paine developed many of Rousseau's ideas, in life and in his writing, being actively involved in both the American and the French revolutions. His seminal work, *The Rights of Man* (1791–1792), became a rallying call to revolutionary action. Predictably, he too was cast in the role of gothic villain, and both his effigy and his books were regularly burned in Britain. Another key philosopher of the 18th century was William Godwin, whose novel *The Adventures of Caleb Williams* (1794) has a classic outsider theme echoed in many gothic texts, although his own carefully expounded philosophy placed reason high above emotions and feelings. Like Thomas Paine, Godwin was savagely criticised by the establishment press, especially when he married Mary Wollstonecraft. Wollstonecraft herself had dared to extend Paine's sentiments to women as well as men in her most famous work *A Vindication of the Rights of Women* (1792). In terms of the gothic, perhaps the greatest creation of Godwin and Wollstonecraft was their daughter Mary, who, as Mary Shelley, would go on to write the most famous gothic novel of all, *Frankenstein* (1818). Tragically, Mary Wollstonecraft died shortly after giving birth to her daughter.

For a while, during the height of confusion surrounding the French Revolution, the term 'gothic' was used as an insult by propagandists from both extremes of the political spectrum. Those on the right accused revolutionary thinkers of unleashing uncontrollable, monstrous forces – horrifically gothic by nature – and used grotesquely insulting imagery to characterise their opponents. Horace Walpole, the gothic author, called Mary Wollstonecraft a 'hyena in petticoats', for daring to promulgate radical ideas of sexual equality. Even more vitriolic was his attack on the French revolutionary Jacobins: 'If Macbeth murdered sleep, they have murdered hyperbole, for it is impossible to exaggerate in relating their horrible crimes; nor can the dictionaries of all nations furnish words enough to paint them in the colours they deserve.' In her turn, Wollstonecraft attacked Edmund Burke's support of the pre-revolutionary French 'ancien regime' with a barbed rhetorical question: 'Why was it a duty to repair an ancient castle, built in barbarous ages, of Gothic materials?' And Burke himself (see page 50) had been one of the main influences on the rise of the gothic aesthetic through his exposition of 'the sublime'.

Such was the confused, confusing and incestuous relationship between the key figures of this tempestuous era, especially apparent in their free use of gothic imagery. Whatever the extent of the confusion, however, it is likely that the seeming coincidence of the gothic with revolutionary upheaval in France – and the threat of its spread to Britain – gave gothic imagery a lifeline at a time when its influence was perhaps already beginning to sag. As Maggie Kilgour suggests:

> Despite its engagement of contemporary issues, it might have been an aesthetic dead end, a one-shot eccentric mutation on the literary evolutionary line, if the terrifying events of the 1790s had not made it an appropriate vehicle for embodying relevant political and aesthetic questions. While the nature of the past, and its relation to the present, was debated throughout the 18th century, it gained new life with the French Revolution, as the Terror proved fertile for a literature of terror. (from *The Rise of the Gothic Novel,* 1995)

The spiritual context

Political and social uncertainties were rife during the time of the gothic revival, and the period was also characterised by immense spiritual uncertainty. In today's more sceptical, less spiritual climate, it is difficult to appreciate the depths of passionate feeling aroused by religious matters in the 18th century. The radical political thinkers, such as Paine and Godwin, were castigated as much for their challenge to Christianity as for their political beliefs; indeed, the two were inseparable in a quite different way from today, when questions of religious belief are generally held to be private concerns. There was in many ways a mounting challenge to the privileged position of the 'official' Christianity of the Church of England throughout this period, and aspects of the gothic revival may be viewed as symptomatic of this challenge – even when unintended by particular authors or artists. In the quotation from Marilyn Gaull (page 5 of the Introduction), the gothic is seen as 'a sudden dislocation, challenge to, or loss of faith in the theological interpretation of nature before there was a scientific one to replace it', and there is the clear suggestion that the gothic emanates from a period of spiritual transition and dramatic change in religious outlook. To many commentators there is considerable validity in this interpretation, although it does appear to relegate the gothic to a mere symptom of change rather than a coherent philosophical stance in itself. This is something like the 'pre-Romanticism' argument already encountered, and again it is a question of informed but ultimately subjective judgement as to what status may be given to the gothic in this context.

In an important sense the gothic revival was a reaction – to a century or more where rationalism, empiricism and classicism were the dominant ideological forces – but this is not necessarily to belittle its power or profundity. The 'reaction' argument is certainly one way of looking at the impact of the gothic on mid- to late-18th century society, and tends to emphasise its over-indulgence in areas of human experience hitherto suppressed. Those artists and writers working in the gothic tradition needed to cultivate certain shock tactics, perhaps, to jolt their audiences out of their lethargy: thus the frequent insistence on horrific detail which many at the time (and since) found objectionable. Alternatively, it is possible to see this process in far more critical terms: a descent to the depths of lurid sensationalism, worthy of the worst excesses of today's tabloid press, as a deliberate attempt to undo the steady progress of society towards an ever more civilised ideal. It is in deciding which of these conflicting interpretations to agree with, or on whether to occupy a position at some point between them, that full account needs to be taken of the historical and spiritual context.

Certainly the growth of rationalism and empiricism had led to a devaluation of religious experience – the mystical dimension of religion, to over-simplify a hugely complex issue – although not of religious belief itself. The vast majority of educated people in the middle of the 18th century believed broadly in the Christian creed, but did not necessarily actually experience God in any immediate, profoundly moving or spiritual sense. If nothing else, the gothic put many of its participants, creators and audiences, back in touch with the supernatural. It is possible to argue, as several influential figures did at the time, that this was a negative distortion of any human spiritual dimension. From a more agnostic or atheistic point of view, denying that this dimension has any reality at all, the gothic may simply have restored mindless fears and superstitions that should have disappeared with the historical Enlightenment during the previous century or two. Christianity itself had developed – and has continued to develop – in such a way as to exclude certain areas of the supernatural from its belief system: specifically the use of 'magic', contact with the dead except through conventional prayer, and the belief in idols and demons. Yet, there continued – perhaps still continues – a powerful undercurrent of belief in these kinds of supernatural manifestation. For better or for worse, the gothic deals with these undercurrents, and in some of its later manifestations – the writings of Aleister Crowley (1875–1947), for example – positively celebrate them. As Clive Bloom has pointed out, 'These excluded areas ... often retain a strong peripheral or inverted relationship with orthodox religion [and] embrace the practices usually termed the occult. In such systems there is a much more direct relationship with the invisible realms ...'. (from *Gothic Horror: A Reader's Guide from Poe to King and Beyond*, ed. Clive Bloom, 1998) It is precisely this 'inverted relationship' which is so interesting, suggesting that there is something profoundly spiritual about these occult beliefs and imaginings even when, possibly especially when, they are opposed to more orthodox positions. It may well be that it is this closeness, almost a symbiotic, twin-like relationship, between the orthodox and unorthodox which led to the most forceful criticism and denunciation of the gothic tendency from conventional Christian believers of the time. The harshest criticism of any idea or movement often comes from those closest to it, as a way of avoiding an embarrassing consciousness of this very intimacy.

Coleridge

In many respects the writer who best personifies this combination of fascination for the unconventional in spiritual experience with a deeply felt need to adhere steadfastly to conventional belief is the poet Samuel Taylor Coleridge (1772–1834). Yet Coleridge is not normally regarded as primarily an exponent of the gothic. Careful reading of Coleridge's poetry and prose works reveals this fundamental and often paradoxical unease. Consider, for instance, his best known poem, 'The Rime of the Ancient Mariner' (1798), which displays many gothic characteristics. In this long poem, the most extraordinary spiritual and imaginative encounters are vividly described in the words of the mysterious, enigmatic Ancient Mariner. Yet, at the end of the poem a relatively tame and conventionally moralistic conclusion seems to be 'tacked on':

> He prayeth best who loveth best
> All things both great and small;
> For the dear God who loveth us,
> He made and loveth all.

The impression is almost of a dutiful disclaimer, putting such strange and supernatural experiences in their proper place.

In his life too, Coleridge was torn between similarly opposing tendencies, which were never quite resolved; perhaps this is one reason why so many of his works remained unfinished, including the most gothic of them all, 'Christabel' (1816) (see pages 74–75). To read Coleridge in the context of the gothic is certainly revealing, for as well as writing verse with distinctly gothic themes, he was one of the most prolific and harshest critics of some key gothic texts. Further, and especially relevant in the spiritual context, much of this criticism is on the grounds of these texts' religious – or, more specifically, sacrilegious – implications. Here, for example, is Coleridge's response to Matthew Lewis's *The Monk* (1796) as it appeared in *The Critical Review*, February 1797, in which he describes Lewis's

> ... endeavours first to influence the fleshly appetites, and then to pour contempt on the only book which would be adequate to the task of recalming them. We believe it not absolutely impossible that a mind may be so deeply depraved by the habit of reading lewd and voluptuous tales, as to use even the Bible in conjuring up the spirit of uncleanness. ... a man's soul had been so poisoned ... that he might extract pollution from the word of purity, and, in a literal sense, turn the grace of God into wantonness.

This is strong stuff indeed; it helps to place the gothic in its controversial contemporary spiritual context, and may allow the modern reader to judge afresh both the critic and the criticised.

Religion and superstition

Writers more central to the gothic revival than Coleridge also provide vivid examples of this combination of descriptive sensationalism on the one hand with an overt moral condemnation of the very matters dwelt on in such detail on the other. In modern media terms, this dualistic approach – profoundly dishonest if consciously carried out – could be likened to some features of the tabloid press, particularly when dealing with the sexual preferences and activities of celebrities, reported in lurid detail but also self-righteously condemned. In the spiritual context of the gothic, this approach frequently featured Roman Catholicism – or, rather, a collection of popular prejudices (all too widespread in Britain at that time) concerning the decadent excesses of the priesthood. In *The Monk*, for example, which has as its central character a Catholic cleric, there is in effect a conflation of Roman Catholicism and blind superstition. Yet, simultaneously, the novel relies precisely on this superstitious element for its appeal, and the various irrational beliefs are never actually disproved in the narrative. As Emma McEvoy writes in her 1998 introduction to the novel, 'The crux of the matter is that *The Monk*, like many Gothic novels, feeds off a Catholic aesthetic, though it takes its morality from its Protestantism.'

Idolatry is one apparent facet of the Roman Catholic faith which features strongly in several gothic novels; another is indoctrination. In particular, the Inquisition is frequently portrayed in fearful terms, making capital, perhaps, out of the centuries-old folk memories of a predominantly Protestant nation such as Britain. The eponymous hero/villain of *The Monk*, for example, had been moulded into his frustrated, repressed and ultimately evil character by the monks who brought him up: 'The noble frankness of his temper was exchanged for servile humility; and in order to break his natural spirit, the Monks terrified his young mind, by placing before him all the horrors with which Superstition could furnish them.'

The impact of education or indoctrination, and the relationship between the two, was in fact fundamental to the gothic world-view, as it was for the entire Romantic movement. The subject would find perhaps its fullest consideration and debate in Mary Shelley's *Frankenstein*, but it also permeates every other gothic novel to a greater or lesser degree. And of course the nature of the education depends ultimately on the view of human nature which underlies it, especially in terms of the spiritual destiny of human kind. The Romantics, following Rousseau, tended towards a view of human nature as fundamentally good – hence their frequent evocation of childhood purity. In so far as the gothic is part of this movement, its exponents shared this opinion. But the reader can never be quite sure: in the gothic shadows there may be something rather more sinister lurking, and frequent gory descriptions of the effects of evil suggest the opposite of a Rousseauesque celebration of innocence.

Gothic literary forms and audiences

The relationship between the urge to express feelings artistically and the form chosen for their final expression is complex, and sometimes problematic. In literature, the relationship is complicated by the use of language – a defining characteristic of any literature, clearly, but also the necessary vehicle for any human thought beyond the basic and instinctual. So the writer, consciously or not, is using a particular form – a form of words, in fact – as soon as an idea occurs to her or him. This form, however, is not accidental or arbitrary; rather, it is determined partly by the nature of the idea itself, but mainly by the cultural and linguistic context in which the writer exists and works. And the gothic is no exception – gothic forms of literary expression are inextricably bound up in the nature of what it is that is being expressed, the purpose of expressing it, the cultural context (including the means of producing and distributing texts), and the intended readership.

Gothic partners: the romance and the novel

That the gothic should take the novel for its primary literary expression is of particular significance. In the 18th century (and for long after; even, in some people's opinions, today) poetry was regarded as the most sophisticated and accomplished mode of literature. The novel, a relatively new form, was emerging from the popular romances published to meet the demands of growing literacy, and the accompanying developments in book production and distribution. The vast majority of critics regarded the novel as distinctly inferior. This was not the view of the general public, however, especially the fast growing female readership. Further, several of the writers associated with the development of the gothic novel were women – notably Ann Radcliffe, Mary Shelley, Jane Austen and Emily Brontë – and the very existence of the gothic novel may be seen as dependent on female readers and authors. In one sense, this may have been a reaction to exclusion from the male-dominated 'higher arts' of poetic and philosophical discourse: the natural desire to express oneself finding a new and perhaps more congenial form which only gradually found critical respectability. But what may have started as a reaction to other literary modes rapidly took on its own conventions and identity in the distinctive combination of traditional tales – often self-consciously harking back to a bygone, mythical past – and a definitively modern form. And here, what Fred Botting has termed 'the feminisation of reading practices and markets' played a vital part. In a patriarchal age, this very fact helped to keep the novel, especially the gothic novel, a low-status art form in the eyes of the critical establishment. Literary reviews and criticism were frequently concerned with the dangers to the female sex of too much lurid gothic reading – in a way which often sounds patronising to modern readers. An anonymous article in the *Scots Magazine* of June 1797, for example, addressed itself to the problem of 'the corruption of the female reader'. The article went on to warn that the reading of gothic romances is:

> ... liable to produce mischievous effects ... some of them frequently create a susceptibility of impression and a premature warmth of tender emotions, which, not to speak of other possible effects, have been known to betray women into a sudden attachment to persons unworthy of their affection, and thus to hurry them into marriages terminating in their unhappiness ...

Fascinating here, as if unhappy marriages were not bad enough, is the thinly veiled threat of 'other possible effects'. The equation of certain types of reading with moral degradation of the innocent strikes a modern note, although the emphasis today is more likely to be on different media than print. But a ready market was assured, and authoritative (male) warnings often only served to increase the attractiveness of 'dangerous' reading.

In the context of the criticism noted above, the word 'romance' was an emotionally laden one, simultaneously belittling the object of criticism and signalling potential moral danger for the innocent reader. Initially romances were genuinely medieval, but these were supplemented throughout the 18th century by contemporary tales of medieval chivalrous adventure, more often than not translated from French (and that in itself was enough to alarm many establishment critics). For some commentators the terms 'novel' and 'romance' were virtually interchangeable. In 1751, John Cleland in a review of Smollett's *Peregrine Pickle*, for example, derided '... romances and novels which turn upon characters out of nature, monsters of perfection, feats of chivalry, fairy enchantments, and the whole train of the marvellously absurd [and] transport the reader unprofitably into the clouds...'. As the century went on, however, other critics began to draw a distinction between romance and novel, with the latter clearly to be the more admired. The gothic author Clara Reeve (1729–1807), in her appropriately titled *The Progress of Romance* (1785), wrote, 'The Romance is an heroic fable, which treats of fabulous persons and things. – The Novel is a picture of real life and manners, and of the times in which it was written.' Eventually, the novel was able to develop as a literary form through a creative synthesis of both romance and realism; by the time Mary Shelley wrote *Frankenstein* in 1818, she was able to describe outlandish, gothic events in the context of a chilling, compelling realism. It is perhaps the most lasting and beneficial influence of the gothic that it was instrumental in bringing about this synthesis: giving flavour and magic – romance, in effect – to a literary form which might otherwise have become marginalised by its own insistence upon social realism as the highest form of literary representation.

Genres: poetry and drama

The novel and/or romance may be seen as the principal form of literary expression for the gothic sentiment, yet other genres are also important. Poetry and drama both played important parts in giving form to the gothic. Varieties of poetry clearly have a close relationship to the medieval or mock-medieval romance in particular, and this closeness is underlined by frequent and sometimes lengthy poetic quotations in gothic novels, either within the narrative or as prefixes to individual chapters, for example, in *The Monk* (1796) and *The Italian* (1797). Given the self-conscious attempt by many gothic writers to hark back to medieval themes and modes of story telling, this fondness for verse is hardly surprising, for the novel simply did not exist in medieval times. Ballads, sung or recited without the encumbrance of having to be written down, were particularly close to the gothic heart, dealing as they frequently did with sensational tales of love, betrayal and death, liberally laced with supernatural elements. Because they were originally passed on by word of mouth, in the context of a largely illiterate oral tradition, ballads opened themselves to wide thematic and narrative variations: a breadth of scope which again appealed to the gothic sensibility with its insistence on a comparatively free rein for the imagination.

The position of drama is less obviously apparent, in that few of the huge number of dramatic adaptations of gothic novels have survived and none has found its way into the modern repertoire. Nevertheless, in the 18th and early 19th centuries, when literacy, although spreading, was still the preserve of the minority, play versions of key texts were extremely popular and helped to bring fame and fortune to their authors. Matthew Lewis, for example, was content to write only the one novel, *The Monk*, and devote his subsequent literary career to writing for the stage – with considerable popular success at the time, but with little or no surviving reputation. Producers of plays went to enormous lengths to achieve sensational effects through stage management, props, fireworks and the like – the equivalent, perhaps, of the efforts of Hollywood in presenting ever more spectacular special effects in the modern age.

With only rudimentary copyright regulations in place, fortune did not necessarily go the originators of the ideas, and it was possible for any one novel to spawn a vast number of dramatic versions with varying degrees of aesthetic or popular success – or indeed of faithfulness to the 'original'. There have been countless stage versions of *Frankenstein*, for instance, starting with the play by Richard Brinsley Peake (1792–1847) *Presumption: or The Fate of Frankenstein* (1823). This play, as its title suggests, gave a particular slant to the narrative and focused on the highly dramatic process of laboratory creation (in the novel largely left to the reader's imagination). For the most successful of gothic novels, dramatic renditions (for both stage and, subsequently, large and small screens) have all but supplanted the original in the popular imagination. The prime examples here are, of course, *Frankenstein* and *Dracula*, to such a degree that recent film adaptations – *Mary Shelley's Frankenstein* (directed by Kenneth Branagh, 1994) and *Bram Stoker's Dracula* (directed by Francis Ford Coppola, 1992) – have included the names of the original authors in their titles, presumably in an attempt to restore some authenticity to these particular versions.

In less tangible ways too there seems to be a close relationship between gothic fiction and drama. In gothic novels there is frequently a vividly dramatic sense of sensational action, often engineered by melodramatically evil characters who seem to play to an audience, at times almost in terms of a farce or even a pantomime.

Other characters also often tend towards the stock parts of melodrama: the hapless, innocent female; the well meaning but imaginatively limited patriarchal figure; the scheming older woman; and the handsome – if not always effective – young male aristocrat. In the form of gothic novels, as distinct from the content, there are also frequent striking echoes of the stage: the multiplicity of short plots, each with its own partial climax within the whole; carefully contrived scenes within scenes presented by different narrative voices; and artfully stage-managed tableaux. This apparently 'formulaic' tendency, with the widely accepted view that melodrama is vastly inferior to drama proper, is not necessarily to belittle the gothic novel. The best of them transcend their own formal limitations, often through a subtle sense of irony about those very limitations. Certainly the gothic writers tended to beg, borrow and steal, sometimes indiscriminately, across traditional artistic divides. But the effect could be liberating. In many ways it is precisely this cross-fertilisation between the literary genres – and between a wide range of art forms such as pictorial art and architecture, as already noted – which again may mark a distinctive contribution of the gothic to the development of imaginative literature over the past two centuries. The imaginative combination of the dramatic narrative, the vividly pictorial and the emotionally poetic may be seen as a strikingly modern breaking down of barriers – a precursor, perhaps, of the finest achievements of the cinema in more recent years.

Production and distribution of gothic texts

Clearly, the cinematic innovation in the 20th century and beyond has only been possible because of the technical progress that took place in film making, advertising, distribution and consumption, to say nothing of the creation of an appropriately enthusiastic audience through direct and indirect advertising. In rather different ways, great changes in the publishing industry in the 18th and 19th centuries had a similarly profound impact on the rise of the gothic. Sophisticated technical developments in the printing industry allowed for far greater, and more legible, print runs than had hitherto been possible, and there was accompanying progress in the means of textual distribution. Taken together, these changes meant that the expanding, enthusiastic readership of gothic texts – and, as mentioned above, the audience for gothic plays – could be more and more efficiently reached.

One particularly effective way of getting hold of gothic texts immediately after they rolled off the press was through privately run **circulating libraries**, to which individuals could subscribe for a fee. Well before the introduction of the lending system of public libraries that we know today, these circulating libraries performed an important dissemination function. Several sprang up across the country, often with a particular textual specialisation in mind. As far as gothic texts are concerned, the most influential and widely patronised circulating library was the Minerva Press

Library, established in London by William Lane in 1773. As the name suggests, this establishment – along with most others of a similar nature – was not simply a circulating library but also a printing press, and in its 1790s heyday was responsible for the creation of thousands of gothic editions. Writers not normally associated with the gothic revival, such as the youthful Leigh Hunt (1784–1859), were avid and enthusiastic subscribers, and the wide circulation certainly ensured that the gothic stayed firmly in the public eye. Influential reviewers, even when generally hostile to gothic texts, could not afford to ignore them, and notoriety spawned by unfavourable reviews in the vast range of reviewing journals only served to guarantee a still larger readership.

There is even an air of under-the-counter pornography distribution in some of the contemporary accounts of the workings of such libraries. Consider, for instance, these words from an anonymous circulating library manager, in *Pratt's Family Secrets* (1797), referring to gothic texts euphemistically as 'good things ... sometimes tricked between muslins, cambrics, silks, sattins and the like, or rolled in a bundle, then thrown into a coach by some of my fair smugglers; the old ones, meanwhile, Mams and Dads, never the wiser'. Observations like these give fascinating insights into the flavour of the times, particularly in the easy dismissal of 'the old ones', and one can imagine many modern parallels. Unsurprisingly, these establishments gained a notorious reputation; Sir Anthony Absolute, a character in Richard Sheridan's (1751–1816) *The Rivals* (1775), declared that 'A circulating library ... is an evergreen tree of diabolical knowledge.' A sense of the irony in these words notwithstanding, there were many, particularly amongst 'the old ones', who were ready to agree with the redoubtable Sir Anthony. With the passing of the intense vogue for gothic reading, at its height in the 1790s, there was a corresponding decline in the popularity of the circulating libraries as purveyors of gothic material. By the 1820s even William Lane's Minerva Press had diverted its attention to the newly expanding and much less controversial market for edifying children's literature. Significantly, in their newly respectable roles such as that adopted by the Minerva Press, circulating libraries continued to thrive well into the 20th century. They included institutions that would subsequently become household names, including W.H. Smith's and Boots, and throughout the 19th century performed a powerful censorship over newly published material: a far cry from their sometimes rather shady gothic beginnings.

Gothic writers and readers

Matthew Lewis and William Beckford

It is hardly surprising that, at the height of its notorious popularity, the gothic idiom provided fame and fortune for some of its chief perpetrators. Matthew Lewis, on the strength of his one novel, was alternately feted or reviled: in either case star status was assured. Such was the novel's fame that author and principal character became entwined in the popular imagination and he was ever after known as 'Monk' Lewis. Other authors gained even greater notoriety on the evidence not so much of their fictional works but of their own lives. William Beckford has already been mentioned in the context of his one major gothic novel, *Vathek*, and his extravagant building schemes at Fonthill Abbey. In his lifetime Beckford was even more infamous for his scandalous lifestyle, which included passionate affairs with older women and younger boys. Beckford's reputation was all the more negative in that he had started life with the appearance of every advantage in respectable society: son of a wealthy Lord Mayor of London, expensively educated , later a Member of Parliament. The death of his wife shortly after the birth of their second child in 1785 perhaps removed the one hope for contented stability in an otherwise tempestuous life. After this Beckford remained in increasingly scandalous exile for twelve years. Although he eventually returned to England, where he transformed Fonthill into a gothic retreat, his notoriety was assured. Beckford dramatised himself as victim, perhaps with some justification, in truly gothic style: 'I have been hunted down and persecuted these many years. No truce, no respite have I experienced since the first licenses were taken out ... for shooting at me. If I am shy or savage, you must consider the baitings and worryings to which I allude – how I was treated in Portugal, in Spain, in France, in Switzerland, at home, abroad, in every region.' Fonthill Abbey became his last paranoid refuge against an antagonistic world, as he wrote in 1811 to his Portugese lover Gregorio Franchi, 'Blessed abbey, save and defend me from such riff-raff and riff-raffery as this! Grow, you forests, raise yourselves, you walls, and make an everlasting barrier between me and them. I shudder even at this distance – horrid, infamous, vile confusion!'

Mary Shelley

For some gothic writers, public interest in aspects of their lives has developed after their death. In the case of Mary Shelley, for example, the actual circumstances of the writing of her first and most famous novel, *Frankenstein*, have been the subject of as much fascination and myth making as the novel itself. The novel quickly established Mary Shelley's gothic credentials in her own lifetime, although she herself, especially after the tragic death by drowning of her husband, the poet Percy

Bysshe Shelley (1792–1822), was most concerned with creating a stable and conventional background in which to bring up her one surviving child, Percy. Nevertheless, the events of Mary's unconventional earlier life, particularly the genesis of the idea of *Frankenstein*, were far more interesting. In recent years there have been two films explicitly dealing with these events: Ken Russell's *Gothic* (1987), which lives up to its title in its use of outlandish special effects, and *Rowing with the Wind* (directed by Gonzalo Suarez, 1988), as well as many pages of print.

The events which occurred at the Villa Diodati on Lake Geneva in 1819, where Mary and Percy Bysshe Shelley were the guests of the poet Lord Byron (1788–1824) certainly provided suitable material for subsequent mythologising, culminating in a competition to tell the most terrifying ghost story to the assembled party. Mary Shelley took the idea seriously, but was initially unable to come up with anything convincing. She later related how she tried hard 'to think of a story', without success. Until, on one particular sleepless night

> My imagination, unbidden, possessed and guided me, gifting the successive images that arose in my mind with a vividness far beyond the usual bounds of reverie. I saw ... the pale student of unhallowed arts kneeling beside the thing he had put together. I saw the hideous phantasm of a man stretched out, and then, on the working of some powerful engine, show signs of life, and stir with an uneasy, half vital motion.
>
> (Preface to the 1831 edition of *Frankenstein*)

This was the terrifying image around which the novel would take eventual shape, and gives a striking insight into the workings of the imagination of a creative writer, and a gothic writer in particular.

This view of the author as almost a passive medium for some sort of supernatural force echoes that expressed by an earlier exponent of the art, Horace Walpole, who told of the process of writing *The Castle of Otranto*:

> I waked one morning ... from a dream, of which all I could recover was that I had thought myself in an ancient castle (a very natural dream for a head like mine filled with Gothic story), and that on the uppermost banister of a great staircase I saw a gigantic hand in armour. In the evening I sat down, and began to write, without knowing in the least what I intended to say or relate. The work grew on my hands.

The process of writing gothic texts, in effect, was beginning to transform the view of the author – a process which would reach its climax in the Romantic sense of the inspired artist in the grip of uncontrollable but profoundly meaningful forces.

Ann Radcliffe

Other writers of gothic novels led less fascinating lives, but still achieved a level of fame and fortune – especially the latter – commensurate with the popularity of their publications. Ann Radcliffe, having written three previous novels which gradually earned her an enthusiastic readership and reputation, was paid the immense sum (for those days) of £500 as a royalty advance for *The Mysteries of Udolpho* in 1794. This sort of money for a novel was quite unprecedented, and demonstrates in yet another way just how popular gothic writing was in its 1790s prime. Three years later she earned even more (£600) for *The Italian*, but this was to be the last novel she wrote in her lifetime. It was almost as if success and a degree of notoriety were too much for this retiring and severely asthmatic woman of letters, and she did her best to eschew celebrity status ever after. She lived until 1823, however, and so completely did she disappear from the public eye during the latter years of her life that rumours abounded of her early death, or, at the very least, insanity. Neither did her elusiveness seem to have been a deliberate attempt to cultivate mysteriousness, in the manner of certain film stars of more recent times, which would have been its own form of publicity seeking. After her death, an admirer wrote of Ann Radcliffe in 1833, 'She had been educated among members of the old school, in manners and morals. A scrupulous self-respect, almost too nice to be appreciated in these days, induced her sedulously to avoid ... her literary fame. The very thought of appearing in person as the author of her romances shocked the delicacy of her mind ... nothing could tempt her ... to sink for a moment the gentlewoman in the novelist.' Christina Rossetti (1830–1894), another admirer, had to give up on her attempt to write a biography of Ann Radcliffe for want of any information on her life. Despite her immense earning power, then, Ann Radcliffe was a rather different figure from certain more recent famous and high earning novelists. It is testimony again to the gothic revival, in a way not perhaps generally acknowledged, that it was able to set a precedent for high earnings amongst popular novelists.

The relationship between the author and the reader

There is a certain paradox in the emerging role and conception of the gothic writer in the late 18th and early 19th centuries. On the one hand, he or she could attain considerable wealth and fame – or both – and become to all intents and purposes a celebrity. On the other hand, as can be seen in the reflections above on Horace Walpole and Mary Shelley, the position of the author as someone in firm control of the material and the processes of creation was being strongly challenged, in effect eroding the power of the individual author. The critic Maggie Kilgour sees this less as a natural process than a deliberate ploy adopted by gothic, and subsequently Romantic, artists to lend a supernatural, inspired air to their works. She writes that:

One of the consequences of this strategy of self-effacement ... is that it encourages a transference of authority and responsibility from the writer to the reader. While the 18th century is often identified as marking the birth of the modern author, it also anticipates his recently announced death, through an increasing shift from author to reader as a centre of attention, and hero or heroine of the act of interpretation.

(from *The Rise of the Gothic Novel*, 1995)

This relationship between author and reader, as it applies to the context of specific gothic literary works, will be explored more fully in Part 2: Approaching the texts and Part 4: Critical approaches, and may be seen exemplified in the texts and extracts in Part 3. One point, however, should be stressed here: the relationship between author and reader could never be the same again after the impact of the gothic – and it is in this area that the gothic played such a significant part in the subsequent development of literature.

The contemporary context

'In the 20th century Gothic is everywhere and nowhere.'

(Fred Botting in *Gothic*, 1996)

Fundamental views of the gothic

As is the case for many movements or tendencies in the arts – and the gothic may be rather more accurately viewed as a tendency than as a coherent movement – there are fundamentally two ways of conceptualising its impact. On the one hand, there is the historical view, regarding the gothic as a particular historical phenomenon which was at its height during the latter half of the 18th century and first quarter or so of the 19th. Taking this view does not, of course, preclude the possibility of self-conscious gothic 'revivals' at other times since; indeed, as has already been suggested, the 18th century vogue for the gothic was itself something of a self-conscious revival of what were perceived as medieval themes and preoccupations. On the other hand, however, is a sense of the gothic which more fully develops the idea of gothic as a 'tendency' in human thought, feelings, and modes of expression, rather than one limited to particular places or times. Here, there is the clear suggestion that the gothic transcends history, or at least permeates all history. It is, almost, a facet of human nature which surfaces in a vast range of artistic forms throughout the ages. As such, of course, its terms of reference will vary enormously, depending largely on the particular context, and even the name 'gothic' need not necessarily be used to describe it. Nevertheless, according to this view, whatever it is called and whatever artistic form it may take, it definitely exists.

The two views are not necessarily incompatible, and most critics seem to be able quite comfortably to take some account of each of them – although the emphasis, inevitably, varies. Richard Davenport-Hines, for example, has used as a subtitle for his important study *Gothic* (1998) the words: *Four Hundred Years of Excess, Horror, Evil and Ruin.* There may of course be a note of irony here, or at least a conscious attempt to attract the reader, but there is also the clear implication that the gothic has certainly not gone away. Other cultural labels conveniently used to define and study artistic or literary phenomena may also be distinguished along the same lines – and, similarly, the two ways of seeing them are unlikely to be mutually exclusive. Differing conceptions of Romanticism – which, as has been suggested, has a close relationship with the gothic – are certainly appropriate here. The same could be said of classicism, the aesthetic outlook which, in simple terms, tends to value form and structure above intensity of feeling, and which is often taken to be antithetical to either the gothic or to Romanticism. For the modern age, in the context of whatever passes for contemporary gothic, both formulations may apply: it may be seen as a self-conscious revival of something historical (with, possibly, elements of nostalgia), but also as a manifestation of an intrinsic facet of human emotional and aesthetic needs.

Contemporary gothic literature

Gothic children

In the sense that this book is primarily about gothic literature in its various contexts, it is fitting to begin this brief appraisal of the gothic elements in contemporary culture with a look at literature. It is apt also in that the gothic in literature has enjoyed something of a revival during recent years, not least in its appeal to young readers. The link between the gothic and the experience of childhood is, perhaps, an especially strong one. As Robert Bloch (1986, in Bloom) has commented:

> On the basis of personal belief and observation, I'd say that those of us who direct our storytelling into darker channels do so because we were perhaps a bit more mindful than most regarding our childhood confusions of identity, our conflicts with unpleasant realities and our traumatic encounters with imaginative terrors.

Macabre features, even – perhaps especially – in young children's picture books, often succeed in persuading otherwise reluctant readers that there is something entertaining to be had from books. In a way there is nothing especially new in this: many adults remember formative reading experiences in which fear played a compelling part, at once terrifying in its intensity and strangely fascinating and attractive. So-called 'fairy tales', clearly, are excellent examples of this perennial fascination – it is hard to think of a fairy tale which does not feature some form of darkness or evil, often portrayed with certain attractive characteristics. Bruno Bettleheim (1903–1990), in his exhaustive but readable account of the meanings and significance of fairy tales, *The Uses of Enchantment* (1976), recognised the profound importance of such reading experiences for a young child:

> Fairy tale motifs are not neurotic symptoms, something one is better off understanding rationally so that one can rid oneself of them. ... Fairy tales enrich the child's life and give it an enchanted quality just because he [sic] does not know how the stories have worked their wonder on him.

This rather paradoxical combination of feelings, neatly summarised in Bettleheim's chosen word 'enchantment', perhaps lies at the root of the continuing appeal of the gothic to readers of all ages: as the Romantic poet William Wordsworth (1770–1850) put it, 'The child is father to the man'. Gothic appeal may even circumvent the explicit intentions of a text, to the extent of actually subverting and undermining those intentions. The cautionary tales so popular in Victorian nurseries, for example, often appealed to children precisely because of their fascination for the naughtiness so fearfully portrayed in both words and pictures, thus working against the moralistic, didactic intentions. Perceptive as ever, William Blake wrote of reading Milton in a similar fashion 'against the grain', explaining (in *The Marriage of Heaven and Hell,* 1793) that 'The reason Milton wrote in fetters when he wrote of Angels and God, and at liberty when of Devils and Hell, is because he was a true poet and of the Devil's party without knowing it.'

At later stages of their reading development, modern youngsters often continue to show a strong liking for broadly gothic elements in their reading. The phenomenal popularity of such series as *Point Horror* and *Goosebumps* is evidence of this strong trend, as is the continuing popularity amongst older children of 'adult' authors such as James Herbert and Stephen King. Once again, in true gothic tradition, adult disapproval (not least from English teachers and school librarians) is a powerful incentive for young readers to read on. As noted previously, there may well be something peculiarly childlike – not childish, which has quite different, generally pejorative connotations – about the gothic: a working out of intensely personal concerns over fear and security, innocence and experience. If this is accepted, then it might account for the continuing popularity of gothic literature. Care is needed here, however, to avoid the trap of simply seeing any frightening tale as gothic. Clive Bloom, in the Introduction to his pertinent anthology of critical accounts, *Gothic Horror* (1998), in fact distinguishes between the two elements of his title thus: 'If the gothic is concerned with the manipulation and exploration of feeling (human nature) then horror is more closely concerned with the manipulation of effect.' This suggests that the gothic approach is subtler and more profound than the perhaps rather formulaic horror fiction so ubiquitous in the modern age. There may be important gothic elements in these narratives – the place of fear in the human psyche and in human experience is surely one of them – but the gothic demands rather more of the reader. And, perhaps because of this, the rewards may be all the greater, especially as a reader's repertoire develops.

Grown up gothic

All this rather begs the question: what exactly constitutes the gothic in today's literature, as distinguishable from – and by implication somehow superior to – mere horror fiction? Perhaps the answer lies in the question, or, rather, in a further series of questions to use in the consideration of contemporary texts, and these issues will be more thoroughly explored in Part 2: Approaching the texts. One modern writer who certainly displays many gothic features in his writing is James Herbert. He has shown himself well aware of the pitfalls of continuing to write fiction in the gothic idiom when so much horror pulp fiction appears distinctly formulaic, and the influence of horror films also seems all-pervasive. In *The Magic Cottage* (1986), Herbert consciously and ironically elaborates on these concerns:

> You've seen the film, you've read the book. You know the one –
> there've been so many: the young couple find the home of their
> dreams, the wife's ecstatic, the husband's happy but more
> controlled; they move in, the kids (usually one of each) tear around
> the empty rooms. But we know there's something sinister about the
> place, because we've read the blurb and paid our money. Slowly,
> THINGS start to happen. There's something nasty in the locked room
> at the top of the old creaky stairs; or something lurks in the cellar
> below, which is possibly itself the Gateway to Hell. You know the
> story. At first, Dad's oblivious to his family going nuts around him –
> he doesn't believe in the supernatural, or things that go splodge in
> the night; to him, there is really No Such Thing as a Vampire. Until
> something happens to him, that is. Then all hell breaks loose. You
> know it like you wrote the story yourself.

Hackneyed plots like this one certainly abound in horror fiction and, perhaps even more so, in horror films. Yet many writers manage to continue the gothic tradition in ways that are refreshing, innovative and say something worth saying about human beings. The modern gothic writer Patrick McGrath notes a particular, dark relevance of the gothic to the modern age:

> We stand at the end of a century whose history has been stained
> perhaps like no other by the blacker urges of human nature. The
> prospect of an apocalypse – through human science rather than divine
> intervention – has redefined the contemporary psyche. The consolation
> that Western souls once found in religion has faded; Faustus no longer
> faces a Mephistopheles from divinity's antithetic underworld, nor is
> Ambrosio (the central character in Lewis's *The Monk*) doomed to
> Christianity's eternal hell. Now hell is decidedly on earth, located
> within the vaults and chambers of our own minds.
>
> (from Introduction to *The New Gothic*, 1991)

Other authors as different from each other as Mervyn Peake (1911–1968) and Angela Carter (1940–1992), Franz Kafka (1883–1924) and Dennis Wheatley (1897–1977) have all in their contrasting ways carried forward elements of the gothic into the modern age.

In the course of this development a certain divergence in the gothic tradition appeared gradually after its 1790s heyday. On the one hand, some writers increasingly emphasised the domestic/realistic in their choice of settings, often with the gothic and horrific elements only gradually unfolding – and, with the most effective writers, all the more chilling for that. On the other hand, an alternative concept of the gothic emerged with the stress on the fantastic: imaginative settings from any time and space and beyond, with few direct or literal links to social reality. Still more writers, probably the majority, combined aspects of each of these gothic traditions. Examples of all three types of gothic writing will be more fully considered in Part 2: Approaching the texts, and in Part 3: Texts and extracts, illustrating the broad directions in which the gothic developed beyond the 19th century into our own times.

Gothic writers: Susan Hill

One modern writer who has been influenced by gothic trends in literature is Susan Hill. An extract from her novel *The Woman in Black* (1983) is included in Part 3: Texts and extracts (pages 92–94). Gothic elements are perhaps most powerfully illustrated in Hill's choice of dark, mysterious settings, against which background struggles between good and evil are vividly enacted. This is clearly true of *The Woman in Black*, which Hill herself has insisted is essentially 'a ghost story', but is also:

> ... a story about evil: about how suffering and grief may warp a
> human personality and isolation compound those things, so that evil
> holds sway, in the sense of malice, bitterness, jealousy and a desire
> for revenge. And evil has great power, on this side of the grave and
> perhaps the other and there are innocent victims of that power ...

This struggle is most famously represented in an earlier novel by Hill, *I'm the King of the Castle* (1970), a bleak but powerful study of the theme. Again the setting plays an important part – Hill herself has acknowledged that the creation of atmosphere is her strongest tool in the writer's workshop – but, in typically gothic fashion, in a way that suggests a particular psychological state: primarily, of fear. Consider, for example, this passage, in which the innocent but tormented boy Kingshaw reveals his fascination for the aptly named Hang Wood:

> There was no question of letting himself off. He had known from the
> beginning, he always knew, though he twisted and turned in his
> mind, trying to get away from whatever drove him. It was what he
> was afraid of, something inside himself which always made him do
> things. Hang Wood. ... It filled his imagination. Hang Wood.

In an Afterword to *I'm the King of the Castle*, Hill has usefully elaborated on some of the themes and has hinted at the method of writing – in a way which connects to ideas of the gothic as somehow being a safety valve for powerful emotions felt especially vividly during childhood. Tantalisingly, and entirely in line with the gothic tradition, her words are more suggestive than explanatory, heightening the fascination:

> That the dark things have their origin somewhere in myself and my
> own past, I do not doubt. But there are Pandora's boxes best left
> unopened, areas best left unexplored and unanalysed – not for fear of
> what dreadful consequences there might be but for fear that in the
> process of laying bare what is secret and explaining it away, the
> treasure trove of a novelist's inspiration will vanish.

The gothic cinema

The same distinction between strands in the gothic tradition in literature, between the realistic and the fantastic, applies – perhaps more powerfully – to the gothic in the cinema. Gothic elements have appeared in a vast number of films made since the cinema gained such an important place in popular culture early in the 20th century. Among the early (and continuing) successes in the burgeoning film industry were adaptations and reworkings of gothic classics: *Dracula, Frankenstein* and *Dr Jekyll and Mr Hyde*. The essential story of Frankenstein, to take the most obvious example, was first adapted for the screen in 1910, with no less a producer than Thomas Edison (1847–1931) – the inventor of, amongst other things, the electric light and the phonograph. Edison admittedly took the rather counter-gothic view that he ought to erase 'all that was repulsive' from the narrative. James Whale's celebrated 1931 version of *Frankenstein* had far greater impact, and established the reputation of the Hungarian actor Boris Karloff, playing the Creature to telling effect. Four years later Whale repeated his success, in terms both of popularity and artistic merit, with *The Bride of Frankenstein*, again using the talents of Karloff, and skilfully integrating Mary Shelley (played, as was the Bride, by Elsa Lanchester). Since the 1930s there have been many more versions, and no doubt these will continue, sometimes wandering far and wide from the original in narrative content or tone, for instance, the comic *Abbott and Costello Meet Frankenstein* of 1948. One of the more recent directors, Kenneth Branagh – who also played the part of Victor Frankenstein in *Mary Shelley's Frankenstein*, 1994 – has commented, astutely, '... these gothic tales seem to satisfy a deep seated fascination with the limits of human experience. They discuss what birth, life, and death mean – why we're here.' (from *Mary Shelley's Frankenstein: The Classic Tale of Terror Reborn on Film*, 1994) Significantly, in the light of contemporary interest in the gothic classics in print and on the screen, in 1999 Universal Studios released a re-mastered video version of a Bela Lugosi film, *Dracula* (1931), complete with a specially commissioned string quartet soundtrack composed by Philip Glass.

Other directors have concentrated less on the classics, more on inventing new gothic creations. In many, the emphasis is on the more socially realistic strand of the gothic tradition, with the undisputed past-master in this genre being Alfred Hitchcock. Although his films are more accurately termed 'horror' than 'gothic' (the two are notoriously difficult to disentangle) there are distinctly gothic dimensions – especially in the characterisation, and in the subtle use of atmosphere to create fear and tension. The more fantastic strand of the tradition has also been well represented, and can be seen to excellent effect in such films as Tim Burton's *Batman* (1989), with the darkly ominous, aptly named Gotham City given a convincingly gothic setting. Interestingly, another of Burton's pictures, *Edward Scissorhands* (1992) combines the socially realistic (the conventional contemporary American setting) with the outlandish (the arrival of the outsider character of Edward Scissorhands, played by Johnny Depp) in a way which imaginatively and sympathetically elaborates on the theme of Frankenstein's misunderstood Creature.

Gothic music

There are some examples of gothic influence in classical music, the most notable being Hector Berlioz's (1803–1869) atmospheric, brooding *Sinfonie Fantastique* (1830), complete with witches' dance, but it is rock music that has been most profoundly moved by the gothic. As with other art forms, there has been a huge variety of different expressions of the gothic in rock music – and a considerable range in terms of quality also. The 1960s saw an explosion of heavy rock activity which had a distinctly gothic side to it in such performers as Black Sabbath and Alice Cooper, the latter in particular deliberately courting notoriety and controversy with outrageous live shows and albums such as *Killer* (1971). The post-punk era of the late 1970s and 1980s was an even more fertile time for gothic influences in rock music and the attendant fashions in clothes and make up. Bands such as Southern Death Cult (later simply the Cult), Outgang, Bauhaus, the Cure, Sisters of Mercy, Theatre of Hate and Siouxsie and the Banshees offered exciting transatlantic variations on the gothic theme – the names alone conjure the type of image conveyed. Mick Mercer, a music journalist, described in his *Gothic Rock Black Book* (1988) the 1980s goths':

> ... violently childish dreamworld, involving immense amounts of energy and play-acting ... Wracked with religious imagery, slippy with sexual inference, Goth onstage is rarely happy. Goth offstage is a hoot. Goth onstage cries, growls and scowls. Goth offstage goes quietly insane and wraps itself in drunken worship, pagan worship, and the loins of psychologically damaged French philosophers.

Revivals in gothic rock music continue to come and go, although not with the same intensity as experienced in the late 1970s and early 1980s. Certainly the gothic lives on in regular festivals, of which more below.

Other gothic media

Mass television audiences have also grown used to popularised gothic in 1960s spoof series, such as *The Munsters* and *The Addams Family*. Both have been repeated, more recently, to large audiences, and the latter has translated into a successful film of the same name. Less comic, and all the more gothic, was the American serial *Twin Peaks* (1990–1992): what one commentator, Richard Davenport-Hines, has called 'the first explicitly gothic television soap opera, with its murk, claustrophobia, evil, haunting doppelgangers, S&M, fetishism and family doom'. Other American series are the cult *The X-Files*, again with a distinctly gothic flavour, and *Buffy the Vampire Slayer,* aimed at a younger audience. British equivalents have not been as successful, although there have been several television adaptations of gothic classics, inevitably *Dracula* and *Frankenstein*, but also such brilliant one-offs as *The Woman in White* (based on the 1860 novel by Wilkie Collins, 1824–1889), and an energetic, appropriately irreverent *Northanger Abbey*. More recently, there has been a successful television adaption of Mervyn Peake's gothic classic *Gormenghast* (2000).

To return briefly to the opening sentence of the Introduction of this book, citing the Internet, it is abundantly clear that the gothic has successfully infiltrated the most modern of media. Not only are there numerous gothic websites, pandering to a bewildering range of gothic tastes from the sublime to the ridiculous and back again, but the computer games industry has also caught on fast. Games such as the *Tomb Raider* series quickly attained cult status, and such is the power of virtual reality that the need for actual gothic edifices, felt so keenly by modern goths' 18th century counterparts, is fast becoming redundant. There are also minority, yet sizeable, cults for other games not involving computers, such as *Dungeons and Dragons* and *Warhammer*, both of which have decidedly gothic elements.

Gothic dangers

There is perhaps a sense that the gothic at best offers psychological, perhaps even spiritual, insights in entertaining ways, and at worst represents harmless bad taste. There is, however, another side. Historically, the gothic has attracted figures such as the Marquis de Sade (1740–1814), whose name lives on in the word 'sadism', and Aleister Crowley, with diabolist associations. More recently, extreme right-wing political movements, often with Nazi overtones, have used gothic imagery to convey their dubious message. In Germany, for instance, the gothic rock band Rammstein was the subject of an article by Denis Staunton in *The Observer* (1999) which noted that:

> ... the band is part of the so-called 'Dark Wave' favoured by many right-wing music fans. Dark Wave fans are known as 'Gruftis', after the German word for tomb, because of their preference for dark, funereal clothes, white make-up and jet-black lipstick. The extreme right-wing weekly *Junge Freiheit* recently explained why the Dark Wave is so attractive to right-wingers. 'If the mystical and irrational, the desire for anti-enlightenment reflection and living transcendence, find their voice in youth culture, the western aesthetic consensus has been breached,' it said.

It is not hard to see gothic elements in torchlight processions, racist cults and exclusive secrecy – some of the hallmarks of Nazism. Politically, the gothic perhaps issues warnings that must be heeded rationally, in context. The alternative, some sort of blind submission to metaphorical darkness, may be dangerous indeed. The relationship between the need to keep a measure of critical distance, and the tendency towards immersion is a particularly important one in the context of the gothic, if only because so much gothic art seductively encourages the latter at the expense of the former. Certainly there is a tension here, and the serious student must come to terms with it; critical distance can enhance enjoyment as well as deepening contextual understanding.

Gothic Whitby

It may seem a considerable step from the perils of Nazism to the setting of Whitby, a small and picturesque North Yorkshire fishing port – but the contemporary gothic, more innocently, resides there too. It was in Whitby that Bram Stoker was living whilst writing *Dracula*, and parts of the novel are set there. This accounts for the continuing popularity of Whitby as a gothic site, with regular gothic festivals involving gothic rock bands and markets for gothic gear, as well as 'ghost walks', the well-organised Whitby Dracula Trail, and the quayside amusement arcade attraction of 'The Dracula Experience'. The town has also been the setting for other novels of a gothic nature, and is well worth visiting for any student of the gothic. To give a flavour of the place, through fictional description, here are some contrasting passages by two very different authors writing at different times for different audiences. The first two extracts are from *Dracula*. The first of these is taken from Mina Murray's journal and describes her increasingly agitated search in a moonlit Whitby for her close friend Lucy Westenra – who has in fact already fallen prey to Dracula.

> There was no time to think of what might happen; a vague, over-mastering fear obscured all details. I took a big, heavy shawl and ran out. The clock was striking one as I was in the Crescent, and there was not a soul in sight. I ran along the North Terrace, but could see no sign of the white figure which I expected. At the edge of the West Cliff above the pier I looked across the harbour to the East Cliff, in the hope or fear – I don't know which – of seeing Lucy in our favourite seat. There was a bright full moon, with heavy black driving clouds, which threw the whole scene into a fleeting diorama of light and shade as they sailed across. For a moment or two I could see nothing, as the shadow of a cloud obscured St Mary's Church and all around it. Then as the cloud passed I could see the ruins of the Abbey coming into view; and as the edge of a narrow band of light as sharp as a sword-cut moved along, the church and the churchyard became gradually visible. Whatever my expectation was, it was not disappointed, for there, on our favourite seat, the silver light of the

moon struck a half-reclining figure, snowy white. The coming of the cloud was too quick for me to see much, for shadow shut down on light almost immediately; but it seemed to me as though something dark stood behind the seat where the white figure shone, and bent over it. What it was, whether man or beast, I could not tell; I did not wait to catch another glance, but flew down the steep steps to the pier and along by the fish-market to the bridge which was the only way to reach the East Cliff. The town seemed as dead, for not a soul did I see – I rejoiced that it was so, for I wanted no witness of poor Lucy's condition. The time and distance seemed endless, and my knees trembled and my breath came laboured as I toiled up the endless steps to the Abbey. I must have gone fast, and yet it seemed to me as if my feet were weighted with lead, and as though every joint in my body were rusty. When I got almost to the top I could see the seat and the white figure, for I was now close enough to distinguish it even through the spells of shadow. There was undoubtedly something, long and black, bending over the half-reclining white figure. I called in fright, 'Lucy! Lucy!' and something raised a head, and from where I was I could see a white face and red, gleaming eyes. Lucy did not answer, and I ran on to the entrance of the churchyard. As I entered, the church was between me and the seat, and for a minute or so I lost sight of her. When I came in view again the cloud had passed, and the moonlight struck so brilliantly that I could see Lucy half-reclining with her head lying over the back of the seat. She was quite alone, and there was not a sign of any living thing about.

Then, in daylight, there are more clues to Lucy's condition, which again mean nothing to her friend Mina:

14 August – On the East Cliff, reading and writing all day. Lucy seems to have become as much in love with the spot as I am, and it is hard to get her away from it when it is time to come home for lunch or tea or dinner. This afternoon she made a funny remark. We were coming home for dinner, and had come to the top of the steps up from the West Pier and stopped to look at the view, as we generally do. The setting sun, low down in the sky, was just dropping behind Kettleness; the red light was thrown over on the East Cliff and the old Abbey, and seemed to bathe everything in a beautiful rosy glow. We were silent for a while, and suddenly Lucy murmured as if to herself:

'His red eyes again! They are just the same.' It was such an odd expression, coming apropos of nothing, that it quite startled me. I slewed round a little, so as to see Lucy well without seeming to stare at her, and saw that she was in a half-dreamy state, with an odd look on her face that I could not quite make out; so I said nothing, but followed her eyes. She appeared to be looking over at our own seat, whereon was a dark figure seated alone. I was a little startled myself, for it seemed for an instant as if the stranger had great eyes like burning flames; but a second look dispelled the illusion. The red sunlight was shining on the windows of St Mary's Church behind our seat, and as the sun dipped there was just sufficient change in the refraction and reflection to make it appear as if the light moved.

More recently, Robin Jarvis has also used Whitby as the setting for his *Whitby* series of novels for young readers, the first of which is called *The Whitby Witches* (1991). The foreword introduces the setting, and immediately conveys the mysterious atmosphere:

Look, look! Down on the sands of Tate Hill Pier; see there, my friend. Three small, strange figures – do you not see them? Listen to them calling to the cliff. Ah, the sound is lost on the wind. But, there, you must see them – they are searching for something. One of them stops and turns to us – its jet-black eyes glare up at me.

It is not quite dawn and the light is poor, perhaps that is why you cannot see. You tell me to come indoors, you say the damp morning has chilled me and take my arm. I glance back; the figures have gone. Can I have seen the fisher folk? The old whalers of Whitby town?

The boats will soon return with their catches. I must speak to no one. I shall let the fisher folk be and try to forget them. Perhaps when I sit by the fire, as my toes uncurl and my head begins to nod, that face shall haunt my dreams.

No, they are but childhood fancies and I am too old. The kettle whistles on the stove and I draw on the pipe which trembles in my shaking hand. Yes, it is a cold morning and I am chilled.

Then, as the story nears its climax, the town is subjected to a series of magical transformations through the witchcraft of Rowena:

Flames crackled up through the roof of the abbey and their flickering light banished the shadows from its walls. The one who had been watching all this time stepped forward at last. Rowena Cooper's bleached hair glowed in the dancing firelight. She raised the staff in her hand and the flames vanished. The abbey shifted through the ages once more whilst below, the town of Whitby jolted into view. ...

Whitby was still lurching in and out of time, confusion everywhere. In the sky the sun and the moon traversed the heavens, wheeling great arcs of light and darkness about the world. Winter and summer mingled in the chaos, trees shrank into the ground and buildings glimmered through the spinning ages. The Norman abbey rose about them. For the briefest of instants they were enclosed within its covered walls, then they fragmented and they stood amid ruins once more. ...

At once the wind died down, the sun slowed and came to rest in the bright blue sky of a hot June afternoon. The hazy images of Whitby stabilised and fused into a solid collection of houses. The harbour was filled with whaling ships, seagulls flew over the church of St Mary and flapped lazily round the cliff, riding the air currents and crying with contented voices. From the streets below, the bustling sound of a busy town drifted up and the majestic abbey ruins shone rich and gold in the sunshine. ...

It was a grey September dawn and the town was waking. Cars lumbered down Church Street and the fish market was about to start on the West Cliff. Just another ordinary day in Whitby.

The real point, however, is that any setting can be transformed into contemporary gothic: it is required only that the writer – or the reader – uses what Coleridge called 'the shaping spirit of the imagination'.

Assignments

1   Making use of the chronology on pages 120–121 and any other available resources, write an introductory handbook entitled 'The Student's Guide to the Gothic' (or another title of your choice). The target audience here is future students of the gothic idiom. This is an assignment best undertaken through ICT, so that it may be added to and amended as subsequent study of the gothic develops.

Work collaboratively, in small groups. It may be best to divide the groups into those undertaking specific tasks and themes, such as:
• historical and contemporary manifestations of the gothic: comparisons
• the artistic presentation of the gothic
• selected quotations with your own annotations

- the social and political contexts
- the sorts of audience – which could feature real-life lovers of the gothic horror genre
- biographical sketches of key authors and others involved in the gothic tradition.

2   Either by means of role playing or through empathetic thinking, explore the continuities and contrasts between historical and contemporary gothic fiction (which may, for this purpose, include film). Working in small groups, if appropriate, consider and list possible questions that selected authors, film directors, and characters from both written and filmed texts, might wish to debate. You could focus on the following areas, amongst others:

- the *content* and *themes* of the gothic
- the *characters* likely to be found in the genre
- the *settings* most chosen by authors and directors
- the sort of *audience* likely to be appealed to
- the differences and similarities between historical and modern wider *contexts*.

The resulting debate could be presented, by video-filming, audio-recording, or 'live' to an audience of fellow students or others interested in the gothic.

3   Carefully selecting your materials, build up a scrap-book collection of quotations, perhaps alongside illustrations, from both historical and contemporary gothic sources (the photocopier and ICT could be useful here). This should give you a vivid 'flavour' of the gothic.

You could follow this up by 'cutting and pasting' portions of text, again perhaps using ICT to assist, achieving an 'inter-textuality' through which both historical and modern expressions of the gothic are juxtaposed, compared and contrasted. Again, some sort of collage of words might be appropriate, using the photocopier's enlarging facility to achieve the right effect for display if need be.

4 Take one of the historical gothic texts (either one of those included in Part 3: Texts and extracts or another of your choice) and consider how it could be re-presented as a modern gothic-horror film. The presentation of your ideas could take the form of:
  • director's notes, including casting, music, setting, and 'mood' creation
  • storyboarding specific scenes or, briefly, the whole story
  • writing the script, remembering that descriptive passages from the original will need to be either deleted, re-presented pictorially, or re-presented through the dialogue.

5 Focusing particularly on children's literature, from early years upwards, make a study – with examples – of gothic and horror elements in children's reading. There are many examples across the 4–16 age group, including:
  • adaptations of classic texts, often lavishly illustrated
  • *Point Horror, Goosebumps* and similar series
  • fairy tales, particularly when accompanied by appropriate pictures
  • books based on films and television series.
  The scope of this investigation could be extended to include children's experiences of the gothic in media other than print: television, film and computer games, for example.
  If time and place allow, interviews with children at various stages of their reading development, as well as your own memories, could add an interesting extra dimension to this study.

6 In similar ways to those used by various writers (two of whom have been featured previously, on pages 40–43) in relation to the town of Whitby, try writing a short piece of gothic prose or poetry based on an area well known to you. This writing may be either narrative, descriptive, reflective, or a combination of these modes of expression. The focus if possible should be on gothic characteristics, perhaps using the contrast or continuity between historical and modern realities as a guiding principle in the writing.
  To further clarify the nature of this assignment, consider carefully:
  • the type of audience (young children, for example)
  • the context (possibly a magazine article, or the opening to a novel)
  • the purpose (to persuade others to visit the area in question, for instance).

2 | Approaching the texts

- What elements might make a literary text 'gothic'?

- How might the various areas looked at in Part 1 actually be represented in gothic texts?

- What sort of similarities and contrasts may be shown by the range of gothic writers under consideration?

Part 2: Approaching the texts analyses how some of the gothic preoccupations and characteristics examined in Part 1 manifest themselves in literary (in other words, imaginative and fictional) texts. A range of different aspects of the gothic will be considered, each related to specific texts, either as represented in Part 3: Texts and extracts, or in shorter extracts and references here. There are more questions posed, as well as tasks and investigative assignments, as the reader applies the background understanding and knowledge gained from Part 1 to a range of gothic texts.

Textual characteristics of the gothic

To consider first the implications of the first focus question above: what elements make a text gothic? Appropriate secondary questions to ask may be:

- How important is the label 'gothic' in understanding the nature of a particular text?

- How may the application of the term 'gothic' either enhance or unnecessarily limit textual understanding and appreciation?

With these considerations firmly in mind, it may be helpful to note some key characteristics. No text is likely to display all of these, and some of the qualities below tend towards the mutually exclusive; nevertheless the list should prompt some useful reflection:

- a fascination for the past, particularly – but not exclusively – the medieval era

- a liking for the strangely eccentric, the supernatural, the magical, and the sublime, sometimes subtly intermingled with the realistic

- psychological insights, especially into sexuality, through (at best) fascinating and intricate characterisation, or (at worst) stereotypical caricatures

- representation and stimulation of fear, horror, the macabre and the sinister, within the context of a general focus on the emotional rather than the rational

- frequently exotic settings and locations, although this tendency may be contrasted to a more 'domestic' gothic tradition, especially found amongst American texts

- plots within plots, often with multiple narrators, and other stylistic characteristics such as the use of 'tableaux' and overt symbolism.

Gothic fascination for the past

As previously considered, the 18th century gothic was essentially a self-conscious revival of something older – or at least a contemporary perception of what was older, for historical accuracy was not of paramount importance. The fascination for ruins and relics permeated all the gothic arts, from architecture to literature, and frequently verged on the nostalgic in its idealisation of the past as opposed to a complicated and unacceptable present. Detailed re-creation of a past era was rather less significant in the gothic world-view than mood and atmosphere, presented through the narrative content of texts, and through the form that these texts embodied. In the range of forms available to gothic writers, the ballad, dating back to an oral tradition, and the medieval romance were significant artefacts. Even more important to the gothic revival was Shakespeare. Indeed it was gothic and subsequently Romantic figures who virtually re-invented and re-presented Shakespeare in ways which are familiar to modern audiences.

The gothic ballad

The form of the ballad, with straightforward rhyme schemes and rhythmic structure, lent itself admirably to gothic purposes. Not least this was through the presentation and conjuring of a bygone age when romance and magic seemed, apparently, to have been accepted as part and parcel of everyday life and were recounted communally in an oral, and often sung, tradition. The subject matter of ballads, frequently revolving around emotional extremes, passionately undertaken actions, and with a vivid supernatural dimension, was also deemed apt for gothic purposes. In the 18th and 19th centuries ballads and romances were discovered, re-created and even forged, so popular did they become. In order to give a fuller flavour of these ballads, two examples are included in Part 3: an extract from Coleridge's unfinished 'Christabel' (1816); and 'La Belle Dame sans Merci' (1820) by Keats. These two poems exemplify the conscious use of the archaic ballad form. There are countless other examples to choose from: many traditional ballads have distinctly gothic overtones and can be found in poetry anthologies, or in recordings by folk singers or groups. There are also several other excellent examples of 18th or 19th century adaptations of the ballad form, including perhaps the best known – Coleridge's 'The Rime of the Ancient Mariner'.

Gothic Shakespeare

Some of the settings and plots created by William Shakespeare illustrate why he was so beloved of the gothic, for example: the opening of *Hamlet*, with soldiers on castle battlements anxiously awaiting the return of a ghostly visitor; the tragic deaths of Romeo and Juliet in the dark vaults of the family tomb; Macbeth's encounters with 'the weird sisters'.

▶ Using your knowledge of Shakespeare's plays, select other examples which you think would be particularly relevant to the gothic preoccupations already noted.

In a sense Shakespeare's position in the English literary tradition is so seminal that every movement, tendency, revival or era uses his work according to its artistic and even social needs, selecting and interpreting as appropriate. The gothic revival was no exception. Quotations and allusions to Shakespeare's plays are sprinkled liberally through many gothic texts: partly, no doubt, to amplify a particular aspect of the story; but partly as well, possibly, to add literary weight and prestige to the work itself. As Maggie Kilgour says, 'Shakespeare often appears as a kind of patron saint of imaginative freedom for the gothic, a voice from a golden age before the tyranny of neoclassicism with its rules and unities set in ... He is the symbol of British aesthetic freedom.' (from *The Rise of the Gothic Novel, 1995*) In fact, it is not necessary to go to the more obvious Shakespearean settings involving darkly tragic events (such as those mentioned above) for the close relationship to the gothic to be clear. Consider, for instance, these lines from *Romeo and Juliet*, in which the youthful Juliet protests the lengths to which she is prepared to go rather than to marry her father's choice, Paris:

> ... bid me lurk
> Where serpents are; chain me with roaring bears
> Or hide me nightly in a charnel house,
> O'er cover'd quite with dead men's rattling bones,
> With reeky shanks, and yellow chapless skulls,
> Or bid me go into a new-made grave
> And hide me with a dead man in his shroud ...
>
> (IV i 77)

Not only the imagery but also the theme – the insensitive, but tragically contested, power of the father over the daughter – are typically gothic in nature. Variations on this theme may be usefully seen in classic gothic texts such as Lewis's *The Monk* and Radcliffe's *The Italian*, among many others.

The gothic past and modern texts

Writers following a broadly gothic tradition continue to be fascinated by the past. Umberto Eco, for example, made full use of gothic conventions and settings in his labyrinthine detective novel *The Name of the Rose* (1980). So too did William Golding (1911–1993) in *The Spire* – centring on the building of a gothic structure. In the writings of novelists like Eco and Golding, there are possibilities of seeing characters and themes more clearly precisely because they are more distanced, and therefore less familiar.

▶ Are there any other virtues in setting a novel in the past? What drawbacks for modern writers might there be in using gothic settings?

Mervyn Peake (1911–1968), author and graphic artist, certainly made full use of the past in his novels, particularly the *Gormenghast* trilogy of 1946–1959 (*Titus Groan, Gormenghast* and the particularly gothic *Titus Alone*). Although not set in any recognisably realistic past age, these stories of incredible gothic imagination make full use of traditional elements, including the oppressive castle and decadent aristocracy, and a nightmarish version of industrialisation gone mad. It is significant that Peake wrote these novels directly after the experience of World War Two and the Holocaust: he was in fact an early witness to the horror that was Belsen concentration camp. Aghast at what he saw, Peake made sketches of Belsen, partly to remind himself subsequently that it was in fact real. One commentator, Davenport-Hines, has suggested that the creation of an elaborate and distant gothic setting was Peake's way of coming to terms with and presenting the evil he saw – '... gothic grotesqueries were his only route to approach the reality of concentration camps'. (from *Gothic*, 1998)

Certainly there seem to be echoes of Peake's chilling experience in his evocation in *Titus Alone* of 'a conspiracy of darkness, and decay; and yet of a diabolical ingenuity also; a setting against which the characters played out their parts in floodlight, as when predestined creatures are caught in a concentration of light so that they cannot move'.

▶ Do you think this works as a way of presenting unspeakable, but real, horror? Can there indeed be an apt artistic response – gothic or otherwise – to the evils of a concentration camp?

The sublime and supernatural in the gothic

Some element of the supernatural may seem to be almost an obligatory component of the gothic. In everyday parlance the word 'supernatural' generally suggests something ghostly, unexplained – and there are plenty of such examples to choose from in the gothic repertoire. On a closer examination, the word itself suggests also a rather deeper level of meaning: beyond or above the natural, rationally explainable world. To turn again to Shakespeare, in an appropriate starting point for any gothic consideration of the supernatural dimension of human experience, Hamlet reminds his friend Horatio:

> There are more things in heaven and earth, Horatio,
> Than are dreamt of in your philosophy

(1 V 167–168)

In this expanded sense the supernatural links with another favourite gothic (and Romantic) concept: the **sublime**. Edmund Burke's *A Philosophical Enquiry into the Origin of Our Ideas of the Sublime and Beautiful* (1757) was a particularly influential treatise in this context, focusing on the human reaction to an overwhelming experience that transcends everyday normality. It is hardly surprising that Burke's words had such an impact, as they succinctly state what so much gothic art was striving for with greater or lesser degrees of success.

> Whilst we contemplate so vast an object, under the arm, as it were, of almighty power, and invested on every side with omnipresence, we shrink into the minuteness of our own nature, and are, in a manner, annihilated before him.

The mystical and religious connotations should be clear; gothic writers also noted the link between this overwhelming, oceanic sensation and 'some degree of horror' (again to use Burke's own words).

Sir Walter Scott, writing in 1827 with the benefit of hindsight about the first flush of the gothic revival, reflected pertinently on the presentation of the supernatural. Interestingly, Shakespeare is again used to demonstrate his case: this time that most supernatural of his plays and gothic favourite, *Macbeth*. Scott was especially concerned for subtlety of expression:

> ... the supernatural in fictitious composition requires to be managed with considerable delicacy, as criticism begins to be more on the alert. The interest which it excites is indeed a powerful spring; but it is one which is peculiarly subject to be exhausted by coarse handling and repeated pressure. ... The marvellous, more than any other attribute of fictitious narrative, loses its effect by being brought much into view. The imagination of the reader is to be excited if possible, without being gratified. If once, like Macbeth, we 'sup full with horrors', our taste for the banquet is ended, and the thrill of terror with which we hear or read of a night-shriek, becomes lost in that stated indifference with which at length the tyrant came at length to listen to the most deep catastrophes that could affect his house.

▶ Do you find Scott's view valid? From your reading of gothic texts, find one example that you feel conforms to his stricture, and is therefore on those terms effective, and one passage which does not.

In gothic narratives there are abundant examples of supernatural and sublime elements described above, sometimes overt, sometimes less so. There is a useful distinction to be drawn between those authors who tend to leave the supernatural element unresolved and those who seek rational **closure** through explaining the apparent mystery. The contrast will be further elaborated on with regard to the nature of gothic horror (see pages 53–54).

Consider this disclaimer from Dennis Wheatley, added as an author's note to *The Devil Rides Out* (1934):

> I desire to state that I, personally, have never assisted at, or participated in, any ceremony connected with Magic, Black or White. ... Should any of my readers incline to a serious study of the subject, and thus come into contact with a man or woman of Power, I feel that it is only right to urge them, most strongly, to refrain from being drawn into the practice of the Secret Art ... to do so would bring them into dangers of a very real and concrete nature.

▶ For the reader, does this sort of warning add to or detract from the gothic nature of the text itself? By ostensibly warning of danger, does this note (deliberately or not) simply attract the gullible? Does an author have a moral duty towards his/her readers in this respect, or should the public simply be left to make up their own minds, without guidance? Should other writers in the selection of gothic texts you have studied add similar warnings? What form might these take?

Gothic psychology

Burke, in the quotation opposite, hinted at the psychological basis of the appeal of the gothic: a deep-seated need in the individual psyche to experience something greater than normal, everyday consciousness – greater, in fact, than itself. The sublime, the supernatural and the horrific may each play a part in this. So too may the relatively modern psychological emphasis on sexuality, and here gothic texts may be seen as pioneering, even if sometimes rather luridly so. Sigmund Freud, the founder of psycho-analysis (that school of psychology which emphasises sexuality as the prime determinant of human activity, consciously or subconsciously), was well aware of the value of the gothic in this context. He felt that artistic creations, literary or otherwise, could tell us a great deal more than could rational explanations about the real workings and preoccupations of the human psyche. In a paper entitled 'The Uncanny' (1919), he explicitly acknowledged the appeal of the gothic, observing that 'the uncanny ... undoubtedly belongs to all that is terrible – to all that arouses dread and creeping horror'. The Freudian approach will be further examined in Part 4: Critical approaches, as will feminist interpretations centring on female sexuality. The tasks below are designed to elicit an awareness and evaluation of the psychological insights contained in a selection of the anthologised texts in Part 3.

▶ Focusing on the following examples, summarise what you think each of the extracts says about the psychological area noted:

• the sinister but compelling attraction of the female figure in 'La Belle Dame sans Merci' (pages 81–82)

• the ambivalent nature of the relationship between the female figures in 'Christabel' (pages 74–75). (You may need to look beyond the extract to a full version of the poem to fully develop this study.)

• the different aspects of sexuality in *The Monk*, including Ambrosio's repressed desires and their eventual distorted manifestation in disgust at Matilda's sexuality and in the rape of Antonia (pages 64–70)

• the relationship between dreams and the psychological state of the dreamers in *Frankenstein* and *Wuthering Heights* (pages 76–77 and 86–87). (Dreams often figure largely in the gothic, and it is no accident that Freud's own work depended significantly on his study of dreaming, as propounded in his seminal *The Interpretation of Dreams*, 1900.)

• the combination of repulsion and attraction felt by Jonathan Harker, the narrator of this section, in the portrayal of Dracula's women in that novel, and the similarly ambivalent presentation of Dracula himself (pages 90–92)

• the study and demonstration of a schizophrenic (psychologically split, to a mentally damaging degree) personality in *Dr Jekyll and Mr Hyde* (pages 88–89).

▶ Bearing in mind the serious psychological insights claimed for the gothic, implied in the task above, consider this rather more critical view which purports to see the gothic in terms of a symptom of mental ill health rather than as a phenomenon that may help in our psychological understanding of humanity:

> Some would say ... that the whole tradition of the gothic is a pathological symptom rather than a proper literary movement, a reversion to the childish game of scaring oneself in the dark, or a plunge into sadist fantasy, masturbatory horror. (from Leslie Fielder *Love and Death in the American Novel*, 1960)

Do you feel that there is there any validity in this view? Try to gather textual evidence, including some of the extracts already considered, for and against such a critique of the gothic.

Gothic horror

The tasks above lead directly to a consideration of the nature of horror and how it manifests itself in gothic texts, for the psychology of the gothic is inextricably linked to its presentation of fear. The two words 'gothic' and 'horror' seem to belong together, so close is their relationship. Horror, however, does not have to be present in a gothic text; neither does its presence necessarily make a text gothic. As Clive Bloom has indicated, 'Horror is the usual but not necessarily the main ingredient of gothic fiction and most popular gothic fiction is determined in its plotting by the need for horror and sensation. It was gothicism, with its formality, codification, ritualistic elements and artifice ... that transformed the old folk tale of terror into the modern horror story.' (from *Gothic Horror*, 1998) The distinction between horror and terror is a useful one here, and was first made many years previously by one of the earliest practitioners of the gothic revival, Ann Radcliffe. In her critical appraisal 'On the Super-natural in Poetry' (1816), she wrote that terror 'expands the soul, and awakens the faculties to a high degree of life', whereas horror 'contracts, freezes and nearly annihilates them'. It is perhaps no accident that in her own novels, Radcliffe tended to explain the apparently supernatural elements rationally, thus ultimately comforting her readers into a sense of security, whatever feelings of terror may have been experienced earlier. Other gothic writers' works are more open to the possibilities of genuinely supernatural elements, portraying and eliciting feelings of horror rather than of terror. Of course any one text may contain traces of both, or even – albeit rarely – neither, and still qualify as gothic.

▶ Read the following extracts from Edgar Allan Poe's short story 'The Black Cat', and decide whether the effect is primarily one of horror or of terror. The narrator of the tale has already described how in a rage he had killed his black cat, an event which set in motion a series of personal disasters. As some kind of atonement, he had then taken in another black cat, but had found a similar hatred building up in him. There is no directly supernatural element here, but certainly a sense of the uncanny.

> With my aversion to this cat, however, its partiality for myself seemed
> to increase. ... If I arose to walk, it would get between my feet, and
> thus nearly throw me down, or, fastening its long and sharp claws in
> my dress, clamber, in this manner, to my breast. At such times,
> although I longed to destroy it with a blow, I was yet withheld from
> so doing, partly by a memory of my former crime, but chiefly – let me

confess it at once – by absolute dread of the beast.
   This dread was not exactly a dread of physical evil – and yet I should be at a loss how otherwise to define it.

In the end, the narrator inadvertently kills his wife, intending to kill the second black cat, but his crime is discovered when the cat, accidentally bricked up with his wife's corpse, attracts the attention of the police search party:

> ... by a cry, at first muffled and broken, like the sobbing of a child, and then quickly swelling into one long, loud, and continuous scream, utterly anomalous and inhuman – a howl – a wailing shriek, half of horror and half of triumph, such as might have arisen only out of hell ...

The same sort of investigative reading could be made of any of the anthologised texts – perhaps the most fertile, similarly combining convincing realism with a nightmarish quality, might be the extract from *Wuthering Heights*. There are also many modern novels which would be suitable subjects, such as:

Clive Barker *Books of Blood* (1985)
Peter Blatty *The Exorcist* (1971)
James Herbert *The Rats* (1974)
Susan Hill *The Woman in Black* (1983)
Stephen King *Carrie* (1974)

Gothic settings

It should already be clear that a gothic tale may unfold against the background of a range of possible settings, although there are certain generic preferences – ruins, dungeons, darkness, for instance. Burke, in his philosophical treatise quoted above, pointed out the value of obscurity, and his words have not been lost on successive generations of gothic writers:

> To make anything very terrible, obscurity seems in general to be necessary. When we know the full extent of any danger, when we can accustom our eyes to it, a great deal of the apprehension vanishes. Every one will be sensible of this, who considers how greatly night adds to our dread, in all cases of danger, and how much the notion of ghosts and goblins, of which none can form clear ideas, affect minds ...

Whatever the setting, some form of obscurity or mystery seems to be a common factor. Consider, for example, the extract from *Wuthering Heights* (pages 86–87), where Lockwood (the narrator) finds himself alone at night in a strange bedroom in the even stranger Heathcliff's lonely house, and then encounters the mysterious, pleading ghost of Cathy. Emily Brontë certainly succeeds in establishing a sense of mystery here, early in the novel. Or look at the enigmatic appearance and words of the raven in Poe's poem (pages 83–85) – and this particular mystery is never fully resolved, remaining substantially obscure.

In many gothic texts, a ruin of some sort seems to embody that sense of mysterious obscurity. In some instances, the setting itself appears to be the main character and gives the novel a title: *Wuthering Heights*, for example, in which characters and setting seem fused together, or *The Castle of Otranto*. In the latter, as Davenport-Hines has commented, Walpole, the author, '... exaggerated his idea of himself by exaggerating his castle. The hero of his novel is the castle itself. ... The battlements, cloisters, galleries, dungeons, underground vaults and trapdoors of Otranto provide the heroics'. In another classic gothic novel, *The Monk*, the monastery imposes itself on the entire plot, attaining the power of metaphor for the intricate themes of the text. It embodies the hypocrisy attributed to the Catholic Church and to Ambrosio in particular: displaying a facade of piety, behind which operate cruelty and repression, in the same way as the apparently holy building hides dark tunnels and dank dungeons.

More recent authors too have emphasised a sense of place as fundamental to their fictions, often borrowing from the conventional gothic stock to do so. This could certainly be said of Daphne du Maurier's (1907–1989) novel *Rebecca* (1938), which revolves around the house Manderley – envisaged here in a dream:

> Last night I dreamt I went to Manderley again ...
> No smoke came from the chimney, and the little lattice windows gaped forlorn. Then, like all dreamers, I was possessed of a sudden with supernatural powers and passed like a spirit through the barriers before me. ... Nature had come into her own again and, little by little, in her stealthy, insidious way had encroached upon the drive with long tenacious fingers. The woods, always a menace even in the past, had triumphed in the end. They crowded, dark and uncontrolled, to the borders of the drive. The beeches with white naked limbs leant close to one another, their branches intermingled in a strange embrace, making a vault above my head like the archway of a church.

After such powerfully evocative prose, mingling sexual and religious imagery, the rest of the novel – its plot and characterisation – can seem something of a let-down. Another relatively recent instance can be found in Stephen King's novel *The Shining* (1977), set in a lonely, ageing hotel which, as Botting observes 'acts as a magnifying glass or mirror for psychic energies and psychotic impulses of certain events and individuals, an uncanny movement in which interior tendencies and external environment exacerbate each other'. (from *Gothic: The New Critical Idiom,* 1996)

▶ Examine again the settings of a range of gothic texts, including those anthologised or referred to here. List the various places, and decide just how important each is to the story that unfolds against the particular background. One interesting way of doing this is to imagine what the story would be like if transposed to a different setting: would it be qualitatively different from the original? If so, how?

As a development of this technique, you could try swapping settings from contrasting gothic texts, imagining what would work well and what would not. Film directors do this quite frequently, using classic texts and re-setting them – *Clueless,* for example (an adaptation of *Emma*), or *Great Expectations,* set in modern London – and it may well be that classic gothic tales could lend themselves admirably to this technique.

Gothic style

Traditionally, the gothic novel has been open to criticism for its apparent lack of cohesion and formal unity. Maggie Kilgour has neatly summarised this view:

> It seems easier to identify a gothic novel by its properties than by an essence, so that analysis of the form often devolves into a cataloguing of stock characters and devices which are simply recycled from one text to the next ... . At times the gothic seems hardly a unified narrative at all, but a series of framed conventions, static moments of extreme emotions – displayed by characters or in a landscape, and reproduced in the reader – which are tenuously strung together ... but which do not form a coherent or continuous whole.
> (from *The Rise of the Gothic Novel,* 1995)

▶ This is strong criticism; from the evidence of your own reading, do you find yourself in agreement or not? If indeed there are 'stock characters and devices' in certain gothic texts, what might these be?

How might other texts with gothic characteristics you have encountered deviate from the conventional, classic gothic ingredients? Do they benefit from this deviation?

Gothic novels certainly often rely on a sequence of set pieces, which could be related to the use of tableaux in drama – indeed there are important links between the two genres. Whether this damages the sense of the cohesion of the narrative is a question each reader needs to decide; it may well be, for instance, that this structure actually assists in the conveyance of heightened emotion at crucial points in the tale. Another structural feature frequently used in gothic texts is the presentation of the plot through multiple narrators, at times telling quite different stories which nevertheless converge on or relate to each other. In *Frankenstein*, for example, there is one novel, but within it several stories. Walton, Frankenstein himself, and the Creature each tells his own story, with the Creature's tale structurally central to the novel and the other narrators successively framing it. In a later gothic classic, *Dracula*, there are even more narrative viewpoints – Jonathan Harker, Mina Harker, Lucy Westenra, Dr Seward and Van Helsing – and the multiple narrator effect is further enhanced by the range of genres used: letters, journals, diaries and newspaper articles.

▶ Select several gothic narratives and explore exactly how and by whom the story in each case gets told. Does the narrative viewpoint make a significant difference to the nature of the tale?

What do you make of the intended fictional audience of the various stages of the narrative? For example, in *Frankenstein*, the recipients of the three tales are Mrs Saville, then Walton, then Frankenstein himself for the Creature's version of events.

In your chosen examples, consider also those characters who are relatively silent. Why should this be so? Would their stories alter the overall effect?

As the gothic tendency in literature developed, so too did the range of structural and stylistic opportunities open to its practitioners. Gothic elements have found their way into a number of literary models and genres, suggesting that the gothic impulse is both fertile and eclectic. Some of the directions taken – many of which have already been encountered in this book and are further exemplified in Part 3: Texts and extracts – include:

- the classic 'gothic horror' tale, with numerous examples already cited

- the historical romance – the *Waverley* novels of Sir Walter Scott (1771–1832), for example

- the American tradition of domestic gothic fiction – some of Poe's tales, for instance, or the novels of William Faulkner (1897–1962) and some of Henry James's (1843–1916) fiction

- fantasy fiction, as in the work of Mervyn Peake or Tolkien (1892–1973)

- the psychological thriller – some of Susan Hill's fiction, for example

- idiosyncratic gothic experiments, as demonstrated by writers like Angela Carter and Salman Rushdie

- some science fiction and science fantasy texts – H.G. Wells's (1866–1946) *The Island of Dr Moreau* (1896) or certain aspects of Isaac Asimov's (1920–1992) novels, for example.

1   Read through – and listen to – any examples of ballads you can find in either printed or recorded form. Using the list of possible gothic characteristics on pages 46–47 as a template to lay against the texts, decide what gothic elements may be present in the chosen examples. Particular areas to consider could include:
    • strongly dramatic, passionately motivated actions
    • extremes of emotions such as love, lust, revenge and jealousy
    • supernatural dimensions for good or evil
    • strong but possibly stereotypical characterisation
    • divergence of narrative point of view
    • a merging of the real and the unreal, as in dreams.

2   Consider what a modern gothic ballad might look like. What sort of events, characters or settings could be appropriate? What, if anything, may be gained by presenting these ideas through the medium of the ballad?
    Try your hand at writing – and even performing – a modern gothic ballad.

3   Research and consider some of Shakespeare's plays in the light of your knowledge and understanding of gothic preoccupations. Try to match selected Shakespearean passages to gothic texts, either from the extracts in Part 3, or from elsewhere. A useful clue might be to follow up textual allusions to and quotations from Shakespeare within some key gothic texts, such as *The Italian*. Does this exercise deepen your appreciation of both gothic and Shakespearean examples?
    Consider how a gothic stage or film director might interpret and present a particular play by Shakespeare (Polanski's film of *Macbeth* (1971) certainly verges on the gothic, for example).

4   Make a thorough survey of gothic textual examples across the ages, noting the presentation and effect of sublime and supernatural dimensions. Any or all of the extracts in Part 3 could be usefully studied here, as could the following (amongst many others you may discover):

Charles Dickens 'The Signalman' (1859)
Edgar Allen Poe *The Fall of the House of Usher* (1840)
Arthur Conan Doyle *The Hound of the Baskervilles* (1902)
Dennis Wheatley *The Devil Rides Out* (1934)
H.P. Lovecraft *The Dunwich Horror* (1945)

5   Try writing a brief parody of any gothic style that appeals to you – perhaps the opening section of a novel.

If you succeed, it is likely that your understanding of the stylistic characteristics will have been much enhanced, for there is nothing like imitation – even if irreverent – to increase insight. There is also a strong tradition within the gothic of effective parody of itself: Jane Austen succeeded vividly in *Northanger Abbey* (an extract from which appears on pages 77–81), as did Thomas Love Peacock (1785–1866) in *Nightmare Abbey* (1818). Both writers' use of the stock 'abbey' setting may offer a hint for your own venture: the setting is vital if parody is to be effective.

3 | Texts and extracts

The texts and extracts that follow have been chosen to illustrate key themes and points made elsewhere in the book, and to provide material which may be useful when working on the assignments. The items are arranged chronologically.

Horace Walpole

From *The Castle of Otranto* (1764)

This is widely considered the first truly gothic novel. The nightmarish fear of being chased by a demonical character (Manfred) is powerfully captured here, and the setting and descriptive detail are definitively gothic.

> The lower part of the castle was hollowed into several intricate cloisters; and it was not easy for one under so much anxiety to find the door that opened into the cavern. An awful silence reigned throughout those subterraneous regions, except now and then some blasts of wind that shook the doors she had passed, and which grating on the rusty hinges were re-echoed through that long labyrinth of darkness. Every murmur struck her with new terror;—yet more she dreaded to hear the wrathful voice of Manfred urging his domestics to pursue her. She trod as softly as impatience would give her leave,—yet frequently stopped and listened to hear if she was followed. In one of those moments she thought she heard a sigh. She shuddered, and recoiled a few paces. In a moment she thought she heard the step of some person. Her blood curdled; she concluded it was Manfred. Every suggestion that horror could inspire rushed into her mind. She condemned her rash flight, which had thus exposed her to his rage in a place where her cries were not likely to draw any body to her assistance.—Yet the sound seemed not to come from behind;—if Manfred knew where she was, he must have followed her: she was still in one of the cloisters, and the steps she had heard were too distinct to proceed from the way she had come. Cheered with this reflection, and hoping to find a friend in whoever was not the prince; she was going to advance, when a door that stood ajar, at some distance to the left, was opened gently; but ere her lamp, which she held up, could discover who opened it, the person retreated precipitately on seeing the light.
> Isabella, whom every incident was sufficient to dismay, hesitated whether she should proceed. Her dread of Manfred outweighed every other terror. The very circumstance of the person avoiding her, gave

her a sort of courage. It could only be, she thought, some domestic belonging to the castle. Her gentleness had never raised her an enemy, and conscious innocence made her hope that, unless sent by the prince's order to seek her, his servants would rather assist than prevent her flight. Fortifying herself with these reflections, and believing, by what she could observe, that she was near the mouth of the subterraneous cavern, she approached the door that had been opened; but a sudden gust of wind that met her at the door extinguished her lamp, and left her in total darkness.

Words cannot paint the horror of the princess's situation. Alone in so dismal a place, her mind imprinted with all the terrible events of the day, hopeless of escaping, expecting every moment the arrival of Manfred, and far from tranquil on knowing she was within reach of some body, she knew not whom, who for some cause seemed concealed thereabouts, all these thoughts crowded on her distracted mind, and she was ready to sink under her apprehensions. She addressed herself to every saint in heaven, and inwardly implored their assistance. For a considerable time she remained in an agony of despair. At last as softly as was possible, she felt for the door, and, having found it, entered trembling into the vault from whence she had heard the sigh and steps. It gave her a kind of momentary joy to perceive an imperfect ray of clouded moonshine gleam from the roof of the vault, which seemed to be fallen in, and from where hung a fragment of earth or building, she could not distinguish which, that appeared to have been crushed inwards. She advanced eagerly towards this chasm, when she discerned a human form standing close against the wall.

She shrieked, believing it the ghost of her betrothed Conrad. The figure advancing, said in a submissive voice, Be not alarmed lady; I will not injure you. Isabella, a little encouraged by the words and tone of voice of the stranger, and recollecting that this must be the person who had opened the door, recovered her spirits enough to reply, Sir, whoever you are, take pity on a wretched princess standing on the brink of destruction: assist me to escape from this fatal castle, or in a few moments I may be made miserable for ever. Alas! said the stranger, what can I do to assist you? I will die in your defence; but I am unacquainted with the castle, and want—Oh ! said Isabella, hastily interrupting him, help me but to find a trap-door that must be hereabout, and it is the greatest service you can do me; for I have not a minute to lose. Saying these words she felt about on the pavement, and directed the stranger to search likewise for a smooth piece of brass inclosed in one of the stones. That, said she, is the lock, which opens with a spring, of which I know the secret. If I can find that, I may escape – if not, alas, courteous stranger, I fear I shall have involved you in my misfortunes: Manfred will suspect you for the accomplice of my flight, and you will fall a victim to his resentment. I value not my life, said the stranger; and it will be some comfort to lose it in trying to deliver you from his tyranny. Generous youth, said Isabella, how shall I ever requite—As she uttered these words, a ray of moonshine streaming through a cranny of the ruin above shone directly on the lock they sought—Oh, transport! said Isabella, here is the trap-door! and taking out a key, she touched the spring, which starting aside discovered an iron ring. Lift up the door, said the princess. The stranger obeyed; and beneath appeared some stone steps descending into a vault totally dark. We must go down here, said Isabella: follow me; dark and dismal as it is, we cannot miss our way; it leads directly to the church of Saint Nicholas—But perhaps, added the princess modestly, you have no reason to leave the castle, nor have I farther occasion for your service; in a few minutes I shall be safe from Manfred's rage – only let me know to whom I am so much obliged. I will never quit you, said the stranger eagerly, till I have placed you in safety – not think me, princess, more generous than I am: though you are my principal care—The stranger was interrupted by a sudden noise of voices that seemed approaching, and they soon distinguished these words: Talk not to me of necromancers; I tell you she must be in the castle; I will find her in spite of enchantment.— Oh, heavens! cried Isabella, it is the voice of Manfred! Make haste, or we are ruined! and shut the trap-door after you. Saying this, she descended the steps precipitately; and as the stranger hastened to follow her, he let the door slip out of his hands; it fell and the spring closed over it.

William Beckford

From *Vathek* (1786)

This novel typifies the gothic fixation with the exotic in terms of setting and narrative: in this instance conjuring the mystery of the orient. This extract is largely descriptive, as is much of the text, and serves to remind the reader of Beckford's extravagant interest in all things architectural.

The Caliph and Nouronihar beheld each other with amazement at finding themselves in a place which, though roofed with a vaulted ceiling, was so spacious and lofty, that at first they took it for an immeasurable plain. But their eyes at length growing familiar to the grandeur of the surrounding objects, they extended their view to those at a distance, and discovered rows of columns and arcades, which gradually diminishes, till they terminated in a point radiant as the sun when he darts his last beams athwart the ocean. The pavement, strewed over with gold dust and saffron, exhaled so subtle an odour as almost overpowered them. They, however, went on, and observed an infinity of censers, in which ambergris and the wood of aloes were continually burning. Between the several columns were placed tables, each spread with a profusion of viands, and wines of every species sparkling in vases of crystal. A throng of Genii and other fantastic spirits of either sex danced lasciviously at the sound of music which issued from beneath.

In the midst of this immense hall, a vast multitude was incessantly passing, who severally kept their right hands on their hearts, without once regarding any thing around them: they had all the livid paleness of death. Their eyes, deep sunk in their sockets, resembled those phosphoric meteors that glimmer by night in places of interment. Some stalked slowly on, absorbed in profound reverie; some, shrieking with agony, ran furiously about like tigers wounded with poisoned arrows; whist others, grinding their teeth in rage, foamed along more frantic than the wildest maniac. They all avoided each other; and though surrounded by a multitude that no one could number, each wandered at random unheedful of the rest, as if alone on a desert where no foot had trodden.

Vathek and Nouronihar, frozen with terror at a sight so baleful, demanded of the Giaour what these appearances might mean, and why these ambulating spectres never withdrew their hands from their hearts? 'Perplex not yourselves with so much at once,' replied he bluntly; 'you will soon be acquainted with all: let us haste and present you to Eblis.' They continued their way through the multitude: but, not withstanding their confidence at first, they were not sufficiently composed to examine with attention the various perspectives of halls and of galleries that opened on the right hand and left; which were all illuminated by torches and braziers, whose flames rose in pyramids to the centre of the vault. At length they came to a place where long curtains, brocaded with crimson and gold, fell from all parts in solemn confusion. Here the choirs and dances were heard no longer. The light which glimmered came from afar.

After some time, Vathek and Nouronihar perceived a gleam brightening through the drapery, and entered a vast tabernacle hung round with the skins of leopards. An infinity of elders with streaming beards, and afrits in complete armour, had prostrated themselves before the ascent of a lofty eminence; on the top of which, upon a globe of fire, sat the formidable Eblis. His person was that of a young man, whose noble and regular features seemed to have been tarnished by malignant vapours. In his large eyes appeared both pride and despair; his flowing hair retained some resemblance to that of an angel of light. In his hand, which thunder had blasted, he swayed the iron sceptre that causes the monster Ouranabad, the afrits, and all the powers of the abyss to tremble. At his presence, the heart of the Caliph sunk within him; and he fell prostrate on his face. Nouronihar, however, though greatly dismayed, could not help admiring the person of Eblis; for she expected to have seen some stupendous giant. Eblis, with a voice more mild than might be imagined, but such as penetrated the soul and filled it with the deepest melancholy, said, 'Creatures of clay, I receive you into mine empire: ye are numbered amongst my adorers: enjoy whatever this palace affords: the treasures of the pre-Adamite sultans, their fulminating sabres, and those talismans that compel the dives to open the subterranean expanses of the mountain of Kaf, which communicate with these. There, insatiable as your curiosity may be, shall you find sufficient objects to gratify it. You shall possess the exclusive privilege of entering the fortresses of Aherman, and the halls of Argenk, where are pourtrayed all creatures endowed with intelligence; and the various animals that inhabited the earth prior to the creation of that contemptible being whom ye denominate the father of mankind.'

Matthew Lewis

From *The Monk* (1796)

Written in the 1790s gothic heyday, and phenomenally successful, *The Monk* was so popular that 'it seemed to create an epoch in our literature' (Sir Walter Scott). In the first extract, from early in the novel, the 'hero', Lorenzo, dreams of his beloved Antonia, only for a monstrous creature to intervene and subject her to his more lewd advances. By the time of the next passage, some 250 pages further, Ambrosio, the eponymous Monk, has come some way to embodying the fantastic creature of Lorenzo's dream, aided by the literally bewitching Matilda. The third extract typifies the anti-Catholicism of so much gothic fiction, and the next shows the further stage of Ambrosio's descent into evil: his rape of the innocent, beautiful Antonia. The final excerpt, from the conclusion of the novel, describes the infernal punishment which awaits the now powerless Monk.

The night was now fast advancing. The Lamps were not yet lighted. The faint beams of the rising Moon scarcely could pierce through the gothic obscurity of the Church. Lorenzo found himself unable to quit the Spot. The void left in his bosom by Antonia's absence and his Sister's sacrifice which Don Christoval had just recalled to his imagination, created that melancholy of mind, which accorded but too well with the religious gloom surrounding him. He was still leaning against the seventh column from the Pulpit. A soft and cooling air breathed along the solitary Aisles: The Moon-beams darting into the Church through painted windows, tinged the fretted roofs and massy pillars with a thousand various tints of light and colours: Universal silence prevailed around, only interrupted by the occasional closing of Doors in the adjoining Abbey.

The calm of the hour and solitude of the place contributed to nourish Lorenzo's disposition to melancholy. He threw himself upon a seat which stood near him, and abandoned himself to the delusions of his fancy. He thought of his union with Antonia; He thought of the obstacles which might oppose his wishes; and a thousand changing visions floated before his fancy, sad 'tis true, but not unpleasing. Sleep insensibly stole over him, and the tranquil solemnity of his mind when awake, for a while continued to influence his slumbers.

He still fancied himself to be in the Church of the Capuchins; but it was it longer dark and solitary. Multitudes of silver Lamps shed splendour from the vaulted Roof; Accompanied by the captivating chaunt of distant choristers, the Organ's melody swelled through the Church, the Altar seemed decorated as for some distinguished feast; It was surrounded by a brilliant Company; and near it stood Antonia arrayed in bridal white, and blushing with all the charms of Virgin Modesty.

Half hoping, half fearing, Lorenzo gazed upon the scene before him. Sudden the door leading to the Abbey unclosed, and He saw, attended by a long train of Monks, the Preacher advance to whom He had just listened with so much admiration. He drew near Antonia.

'And where is the Bridegroom?' said the imaginary Friar.

Antonia seemed to look round the Church with anxiety. Involuntarily the Youth advanced a few steps from his concealment. She saw him; The blush of pleasure glowed upon her cheek; With a graceful motion of her hand She beckoned to him to advance. He disobeyed not the command; He flew towards her, and threw himself at her feet.

She retreated for a moment; Then gazing upon him with unutterable delight;—'Yes !' She exclaimed, 'My Bridegroom! My destined Bridegroom !'

She said, and hastened to throw herself into his arms; But before He had time to receive her, an Unknown rushed between them. His form was gigantic, His complexion was swarthy, His eyes fierce and terrible; his Mouth breathed out volumes of fire; and on his forehead was written in legible characters—'Pride! Lust! Inhumanity!'

Antonia shrieked. The Monster clasped her in his arms, and springing with her upon the Altar, tortured her with his odious caresses. She endeavoured in vain to escape from his embrace. Lorenzo flew to her succour, but ere He had time to reach her, a loud burst of thunder was heard. Instantly the Cathedral seemed crumbling into pieces; The Monks betook themselves to flight, shrieking fearfully; The Lamps were extinguished, the Altar sank down, and in its place appeared an abyss vomiting forth clouds of flame. Uttering a loud and terrible cry the Monster plunged into the Gulph, and in his fall attempted to drag Antonia with him. He strove in vain. Animated by supernatural powers She disengaged herself from his embrace; But her white Robe left in his possession. Instantly a wing of brilliant splendour spread itself from either of Antonia's arms. She darted upwards, and while ascending cried to Lorenzo,

'Friend! we shall meet above!'

At the same moment the Roof of the Cathedral opened; Harmonious voices pealed along the Vaults, and the glory into which Antonia was received, was composed of rays of such dazzling brightness, that Lorenzo was unable to sustain the gaze. His sight failed, and He sank upon the ground.

*   *   *   *   *   *   *   *

It was now that Ambrosio repented of his rashness. The solemn singularity of the charm had prepared him for something strange and horrible. He waited with fear for the Spirit's appearance, whose coming was announced by thunder and earthquakes. He looked wildly round him, expecting that some dreadful Apparition would meet his eyes, the sight of which would drive him mad. A cold shivering seized his body, and He sank upon one knee, unable to support himself.

'He comes!' exclaimed Matilda in a joyful accent.

Ambrosio started, and expected the Dæmon with terror. What was his surprise, when the Thunder ceasing to roll, a full strain of melodious Music sounded in the air. At the same time the cloud dispersed, and He beheld a Figure more beautiful, than Fancy's pencil ever drew. It was a Youth seemingly scarce eighteen, the perfection of whose form and face was unrivalled. He was perfectly naked: A bright Star sparkled upon his fore-head; Two crimson wings extended themselves from his shoulders; and his silken locks were confined by a band of many-coloured fires, which played round his head, formed themselves into a variety of figures, and shone with a brilliance far surpassing that of precious Stones. Circlets of diamonds were fastened round his arms and ankles, and in his right hand He bore a silver branch, imitating Myrtle. His form shone with dazzling glory: He was surrounded by clouds of rose-coloured light, and at the moment that He appeared, a refreshing air breathed perfumes through the Cavern. Enchanted at a vision so contrary to his expectations, Ambrosio gazed upon the Spirit with delight and wonder: Yet however beautiful the Figure, He could not but remark a wildness in the Dæmon's eyes, and a mysterious melancholy impressed upon his features, betraying the Fallen Angel, and inspiring the Spectators with secret awe.

The Music ceased. Matilda addressed herself to the Spirit. She spoke in a language unintelligible to the Monk, and was answered in the same. She seemed to insist upon something, which the Dæmon was unwilling to grant. He frequently darted upon Ambrosio angry glances, and at such time the Friar's heart sank within him. Matilda appeared to grow incensed. She spoke in a loud and commanding tone, and her gestures declared, that She was threatening him with her vengeance. Her menaces had the desired effect: The Spirit sank upon his knee, and with a submissive air presented to her the branch of Myrtle. No sooner had She received it, than the Music was again heard. A thick cloud spread itself over the Apparition, The blue flames disappeared, and total obscurity reigned through the Cave. The Abbot moved not from his place. His faculties were all bound up in pleasure, anxiety, and surprise. At length the darkness dispersing, He perceived Matilda standing hear him in her religious habit, with the Myrtle in her hand. No traces of the incantation, and the Vaults were only illuminated by the faint rays of the sepulchral Lamp.

*   *   *   *   *   *   *   *

The Nuns were employed in religious duties established in honour of St. Clare, and to which no Prophane was ever admitted. The Chapel-windows were illuminated. As they stood on the outside, the Auditors heard the full swell of the organ, accompanied by a chorus of female voices, rise upon the stillness of the night. This died away, and was succeeded by a single strain of harmony. It was the voice of her who was destined to sustain in the procession the characters of St. Clare. For the office the most beautiful Virgin of Madrid was always selected, and She upon whom the choice fell, esteemed it as the highest of honours. While listening to the Music, whose melody distance only seemed to render sweeter, the audience was wrapped up in profound attention. Universal silence prevailed through the Crowd, and every heart was filled with reverence for religion. Every heart but Lorenzo's. Conscious that among those who chuanted the praises of their God so sweetly, there were some who cloaked with devotion the foulest sins, their hymns inspired him with detestation at their Hypocrisy. He had long observed with disapprobation and contempt the superstition, which governed Madrid's Inhabitants. His good sense had pointed out to him the artifices of the Monks, and the gross absurdity of their miracles, wonders and supposititious reliques. He blushed to see his Countrymen the Dupes of deceptions so ridiculous, and only wished for an opportunity to free them from their monkish fetters. That opportunity, so long desired in vain, was at length presented to him. He resolved not to let it slip, but to set before the People in glaring colours, how enormous were the abuses but too frequently practised in Monasteries, and how unjustly public esteem was bestowed indiscriminately upon all who wore a religious habit. He longed for the moment destined to unmask the Hypocrites, and convince his Countrymen, that a sanctified exterior does not always hide a virtuous heart.

        *   *   *   *   *   *   *   *

With every moment the Friar's passion became more ardent, and Antonia's terror more intense. She struggled to disengage herself from his arms. Her exertions were unsuccessful; and finding that Ambrosio's conduct became still freer. She shrieked for assistance with all her strength. The aspect of the Vault, the pale glimmering of the Lamp, the surrounding obscurity, the sight of the Tomb, and the objects of mortality which met her eyes of either side, were ill-calculated to inspire her with those emotions, by which the Friar was agitated. Even his caresses terrified her from their fury, and created no other sentiment than fear. On the contrary, her alarm, her evident disgust, and incessant opposition, seemed only to inflame the Monk's desires, and supply his brutality with additional strength. Antonia's shrieks were unheard. Yet She continued them, nor abandoned her endeavours to escape, till exhausted and out of breath She sank from his arms upon her knees, and once more had recourse to prayers and supplications. This attempt had no better success than the former. On the contrary, taking advantage of her situation, the Ravisher threw himself by her side. He clasped her to his bosom almost lifeless with terror, and faint with struggling. He stifled her cries with kisses, treated her with the rudeness of an unprincipled Barbarian, proceeded from freedom to freedom, and in the violence of his lustful delirium, wounded and bruised her tender limbs. Heedless of her tears, cries and entreaties, He gradually made himself Master of her person, and desisted not from his prey, till He had accomplished his crime and the dishonour of Antonia.

Scarcely had He succeeded in his design, than He shuddered at himself and the means by which it was effected. The very excess of his former eagerness to possess Antonia now contributed to inspire him with disgust; and a secret impulse made him feel, how base and unmanly was the crime, which He had just committed. He started hastily from her arms. She, who had so lately been the object of his adoration, now raised no other sentiment in his heart than aversion and rage. He turned away from her; or if his eyes rested upon her figure involuntarily, it was only to dart upon her looks of hate. The Unfortunate had fainted ere the completion of her disgrace: She only recovered life to be sensible of her misfortune. She remained stretched upon the earth in silent despair: The tears chased each other slowly down her cheeks, and her bosom heaved with frequent sobs. Oppressed with grief, She continued for some time in this state of torpidity. At length She rose with difficulty, and dragging her feeble steps towards the door, prepared to quit the dungeon.

*   *   *   *   *   *   *   *

The Fiend answered with a malicious laugh:

'Our contract? Have I not performed my part? What more did I promise than to save you from your prison? Have I not done so? Are you not safe from the Inquisition—safe from all but from me? Fool that you were to confide yourself to a Devil! Why did you not stipulate for life, and power, and pleasure? Then all would have been granted: Now your reflections come too late. Miscreant, prepare for death; You have not many hours to live!'

On hearing this sentence, dreadful were the feelings of the devoted Wretch! He sank upon his knees, and raised his hands towards heaven. The Fiend read his intention and prevented it—

'What?' He cried, darting at him a look of fury: 'Dare you still implore the Eternal's mercy? Would you feign penitence, and again act an Hypocrite's part? Villain, resign your hopes of pardon. Thus I secure my prey!'

As He said this, darting his talons into the Monk's shaven crown, He sprang with him from the rock. The Caves and mountains rang with Ambrosio's shrieks. The Dæmon continued to soar aloft, till reaching a dreadful height, He released the sufferer. Headlong fell the Monk through the airy waste; and He rolled from precipice to precipice, till bruised and mangled He rested on the river's banks. Life still existed in his miserable frame. He attempted in vain to raise himself; His broken and dislocated limbs refused to perform their office, nor was He able to quit the post where He had first fallen. The sun now rose above the horizon; Its scorching beams darted full upon the head of the expiring Sinner. Myriads of insects were called forth by the warmth. They drank the blood which trickled from Ambrosio's wounds. He had no power to drive them from him, and they fastened upon his sores, darted their stings into his body, covered him with their multitudes, and inflicted on him tortures the most exquisite and insupportable. The Eagles of the rock tore his flesh piecemeal, and dug out his eye-balls with their crooked beaks. A burning thirst tormented him; He heard the river's murmur as it rolled beside him, but strove in vain to drag himself towards the sound. Blind, maimed, helpless, and despairing, venting his rage in blasphemy and curses, execrating his existence, yet dreading the arrival of death destined to yield him up to greater torments, six miserable days did the Villain languish. On the Seventh a violent storm arose: The winds in fury rent up rocks and forests: The sky was now black with clouds, now sheeted with fire: The rain fell in torrents; It swelled the stream; The waves overflowed their banks; They reached the spot where Ambrosio lay, and when they abated carried with them into the river the Corse of the despairing Monk.

Ann Radcliffe

From *The Italian* (1797)

Ann Radcliffe's novel may be seen as something of a riposte to *The Monk*, which she saw as excessively horrific. Certainly *The Italian* is milder, but it has its moments: the first extract helps create the rather eerie atmosphere; the second is laden with typically gothic intimations of doom and despair, despite the actual setting of Vivaldi's wedding.

Vivaldi again examined the walls, and as unsuccessfully as before; but in one corner of the vault lay an object, which seemed to tell the fate of one who had been confined here, and to hint his own: it was a garment covered with blood. Vivaldi and his servant discovered it at the same instant; and a dreadful foreboding of their own destiny fixed them, for some moments, to the spot. Vivaldi first recovered himself, when instead of yielding to despondency, all his faculties were aroused to devise some means for escaping; but Paulo's hopes seemed buried beneath the dreadful vestments upon which he still gazed. 'Ah, my Signor!' said he, at length, in a faultering accent, 'who shall dare to raise that garment? What if it should conceal the mangled body whose blood has stained it!'

Vivaldi, shudderingly, turned to look on it again.

'It moves!' exclaimed Paulo; 'I see it move!' as he said which, he started to the opposite side of the chamber. Vivaldi stepped a few paces back, and as quickly returned; when, determined to know the event at once, he raised the garment upon the point of his sword, and perceived, beneath, other remains of dress, heaped high together, while even the floor below was stained with gore.

Believing that fear had deceived the eyes of Paulo, Vivaldi watched this horrible spectacle for some time, but without perceiving the least motion; when he became convinced, that not any remains of life were shrouded beneath it, and that it contained only articles of dress, which had belonged to some unfortunate person, who had probably been decoyed hither for plunder, and afterwards murdered. This belief, and the repugnance he felt to dwell upon the spectacle, prevented him from examining further, and he turned away to a remote part of the vault. A conviction of his own fate and of his servant's filled his mind for a while with despair. It appeared that he had been ensnared by robbers, till, as he recollected the circumstances which had attended his entrance, and the several peculiar occurrences connected with the arch-way this conjecture seemed highly improbable. It was unreasonable, that robbers should have taken the trouble to decoy, when they might at first have seized him; still more so, that they would have persevered so long in the attempt; and most of all, that when he had formerly been in their power, they should have neglected their opportunity, and suffered him to leave the ruin unmolested. Yet granting that all this, improbable as it was, were, however, possible, the solemn warnings and predictions of the monk, so frequently delivered, and so faithfully fulfilled, could have no connection with the schemes of banditti. It appeared, therefore, that Vivaldi was not in the hands of robbers; or, if he were, that the monk, at least, had no connection with them; yet it was certain that he had just heard the voice of this monk beneath the arch; that his servant had said, he saw the vestments of one ascending the steps of the fort; and that they had both reason, afterward, to believe it was his shadowy figure which they had pursued to the very chamber where they were now confined.

As Vivaldi considered all these circumstances, his perplexity encreased and he was more than ever inclined to believe, that the form, which had assumed the appearance of a monk, was something superhuman.

'If this being had *appeared only*,' said he to himself, 'I should, perhaps, have thought it the perturbed spirit of him, who doubtless has been murdered here, and that it led me hither to discover the deed, that his bones might be removed to holy ground; but this monk, or whatever it is, was neither silent, nor apparently anxious concerning himself; he spoke only of events connected with my peace, and predicted of the future, as well as reverted to the past! If he had either hinted of himself, or had been wholly silent, his appearance, and manner of eluding pursuit, is so extraordinary, that I should have yielded, for once, perhaps, to the tales of our grandfathers, and thought he was the spectre of a murdered person.'

As Vivaldi expressed his incredulity, however, he returned to examine the garment once more, when, as he raised it, he observed, what had before escaped his notice, black drapery mingled with the heap beneath; and, on lifting this also on the point of his sword, he perceived part of the habiliment of a monk! He started at the discovery, as if he had seen the apparition, which had so long been tempting his credulity. Here were the vest and scapulary, rent and stained with blood! Having gazed for a moment, he let them drop upon the heap; when Paulo, who had been silently observing him, exclaimed,

'Signor! that should be the garment of the demon who led us hither. Is it a winding-sheet for us, Maestro? Or was it one for the body he inhabited while on earth!'

*   *   *   *   *   *   *   *

As the appointed hour drew near, her spirits sunk, and she watched with melancholy foreboding, the sun retiring amidst stormy clouds, and his rays fading from the highest points of the mountains, till the gloom of twilight prevailed over the scene. She then left her apartment, took a grateful leave of the hospitable Abbess, and attended by the lay-sister, quitted the convent.

Immediately without the gate she was met by Vivaldi, whose look, as he put her arm within his, gently reproached her for the dejection of her air.

They walked in silence towards the chapel of San Sebastian. The scene appeared to sympathize with the spirit of Ellena. It was a gloomy evening, and the lake, which broke in dark waves upon the shore, mingled its hollow sounds with those of the wind, that bowed the lofty pines, and swept in gusts among the rocks. She observed with alarm the heavy thunder clouds, that rolled along the sides of the mountains, and the birds circling swiftly over the waters, and scudding away to their nests among the cliffs; and she noticed to Vivaldi, that, as a storm seemed approaching, she wished to avoid crossing the lake. He immediately ordered Paulo to dismiss the boat, and to be in waiting with a carriage, that, if the weather should become clear, they might not be detained longer than was otherwise necessary.

As they approached the chapel, Ellena fixed her eyes on the mournful cypresses which waved over it, and sighed. 'Those,' she said, 'are funereal mementos—not such as should grace the altar of marriage! Vivaldi, I could be superstitious.—Think you not they are portentous of future misfortune? But forgive me; my spirits are weak.'

Vivaldi endeavoured to soothe her mind, and tenderly reproached her for the sadness she indulged. Thus they entered the chapel. Silence, and a kind of gloomy sepulchral light, prevailed within. The venerable Benedictine, with a brother, who was to serve as guardian to the bride, were already there, but they were kneeling, and engaged in prayer.

Vivaldi led the trembling Ellena to the altar, where they waited till the Benedictines should have finished, and these were moments of great emotion. She often looked round the dusky chapel, in fearful expectation of discovering some lurking observer, and, though she knew it to be very improbable, that any person in this neighbourhood could be interested in interrupting the ceremony, her mind involuntarily admitted the possibility of it. Once, indeed, as her eyes glanced over a casement, Ellena fancied she distinguished a human face laid close to the glass, as if to watch what was passing within; but when she looked again, the apparition was gone. Notwithstanding this, she listened with anxiety to the uncertain sounds without, and sometimes started as the surges of the lake dashed over the rock below, almost believing she heard the steps and whispering voices of men in the avenues of the chapel. She tried, however, to subdue apprehension, by considering, that if this were true, an harmless curiosity might have attracted some inhabitants of the convent hither, and her spirits became more composed, till she observed a door open a little way, and a dark countenance looking from behind it. In the next instant it retreated, and the door was closed.

Samuel Taylor Coleridge

From 'Christabel' (1816)

This is the opening of Coleridge's unfinished poem, setting the scene and introducing the chief characters – including the ominously, but attractively, mysterious Geraldine. The theme of seduction and subsequent corruption of innocence, through the agency of magic, has a strongly gothic dimension.

'Tis the middle of night by the castle clock,
And the owls have awakened the crowing cock;
Tu—whit!——To—Whoo!
And hark, again! the crowing cock,
How drowsily it crew.
Sir Leoline, the Baron rich,
Hath a toothless mastiff bitch;
From her kennel beneath the rock
She maketh answer to the clock,
Four for the quarters, and twelve for the hour;
Ever and aye, by shine and shower,
Sixteen short howls, not over loud;
Some say, she sees my lady's shroud.

Is the night chilly and dark?
The night is chilly but not dark.
The thin gray cloud is spread on high,
It covers but not hides the sky.
The moon is behind, and at the full;
And yet she looks both small and dull.
The night is chill, the cloud is gray:
'Tis a month before the month of May,
And the Spring comes slowly up this way.

The lovely lady, Christabel,
Whom her father loves so well,
What makes her in the wood so late,
A furlong from the castle gate?
She had dreams all yesternight
Of her own betrothéd knight;
And she in the midnight wood will pray
For the weal of her lover that's far away.

She stole along, she nothing spoke,
The sighs she heaved were soft and low,
And naught was green upon the oak
But moss and rarest mistletoe:
She kneels beneath the huge oak tree,
And in silence prayeth she.

The lady sprang up suddenly,
The lovely lady, Christabel!
It moaned as near, as near can be,
But what it is she cannot tell.—
On the other side it seems to be,
Of the huge, broad-breasted, old oak tree.

The night is chill; the forest bare;
Is it the wind that moaneth bleak?
There is not wind enough in the air
To move away the ringlet curl
From the lovely lady's cheek—
There is not wind enough to twirl
The one red leaf, the last if its clan,
That dances as often as dance it can,
Hanging so light, and hanging so high,
On the topmost twig that looks up at the sky.

Hush, beating heart of Christabel!
Jesu, Maria, shield her well!
She folded her arms beneath her cloak,
And stole to the other side of the oak.
                What sees she there?

There she sees a damsel bright,
Drest in a silken robe of white,
That shadowy in the moonlight shone:
The neck that made that white robe wan,
Her stately neck, and arms were bare;
Her blue-veined feet unsandal'd were,
And wildly glittered here and there
The gems entangled in her hair.
I guess, 'twas frightful there to see
A lady so richly clad as she–
Beautiful exceedingly!

Mary Shelley

From *Frankenstein* (1818)

Frankenstein is of course one of the most famous gothic novels, and has been referred to many times in this book. Here, Frankenstein beholds with horror the fruits of his labours: the unnamed Creature. His subsequent dream, mingling disgust with desire, is also quintessentially gothic.

It was on a dreary night of November that I beheld the accomplishment of my toils. With an anxiety that almost amounted to agony, I collected the instruments of life around me, that I might infuse a spark of being into the lifeless thing that lay at my feet. It was already one in the morning; the rain pattered dismally against the panes, and my candle was nearly burnt out, when, by the glimmer of the half-extinguished light, I saw the dull yellow eye of the creature open; it breathed hard, and a convulsive motion agitated its limbs.

How can I describe my emotions at this catastrophe, or how delineate the wretch whom with such infinite pains and care I had endeavoured to form? His limbs were in proportion, and I had selected his features as beautiful. Beautiful! – Great God! His yellow skin scarcely covered the work of muscles and arteries beneath; his hair was of a lustrous black, and flowing; his teeth of a pearly whiteness; but these luxuriances only formed a more horrid contrast with his watery eyes, that seemed almost of the same colour as the dun white sockets in which they were set, his shrivelled complexion and straight black lips.

The different accidents of life are not so changeable as the feelings of human nature. I had worked hard for nearly two years, for the sole purpose of infusing life into an inanimate body. For this I had deprived myself of rest and health. I had desired it with an ardour that far exceeded moderation; but now that I had finished, the beauty of the dream vanished, and breathless horror and disgust filled my heart. Unable to endure the aspect of the being I had created, I rushed out of the room, and continued a long time traversing my bedchamber, unable to compose my mind to sleep. At length lassitude succeeded to the tumult I had before endured; and I threw myself on the bed in my clothes, endeavouring to seek a few moments of forgetfulness. But it was in vain: I slept, indeed, but I was disturbed by the wildest dreams. I thought I saw Elizabeth, in the bloom of health, walking in the streets of Ingolstadt. Delighted and surprised, I embraced her; but as I imprinted the first kiss on her lips, they became livid with the hue of death; her features appeared to change, and I thought that I held the corpse of my dead mother in my arms; a shroud enveloped her form, and I saw the grave-worms crawling in the folds of the flannel. I started from my sleep with horror; a cold dew covered my forehead, my teeth chattered, and every limb became convulsed: when, by the dim and yellow light of the moon, as it forced its way through the window shutters, I beheld the wretch – the miserable monster whom I had created. He held up the curtain of the bed; and his eyes, if eyes they may be called, were fixed on me. His jaws opened, and he muttered some inarticulate sounds, while a grin wrinkled his cheeks. He might have spoken, but I did not hear; one hand was stretched out, seemingly to detain me, but I escaped, and rushed down stairs. I took refuge in the courtyard belonging to the house which I inhabited; where I remained during the rest of the night, walking up and down in the greatest agitation, listening attentively, catching and fearing each sound as if it were to announce the approach of the demoniacal corpse to which I had so miserably given life.

Oh! no mortal could support the horror of that countenance. A mummy again endued with animation could not be so hideous as that wretch. I had gazed on him while unfinished; he was ugly then; but when those muscles and joints were rendered capable of motion, it became a thing such as even Dante could not have conceived.

I passed the night wretchedly. Sometimes my pulse beat so quickly and hardly that I felt the palpitation of every artery; at others, I nearly sank to the ground through languor and extreme weakness. Mingled with this horror, I felt the bitterness of disappointment; dreams that had been my food and pleasant rest for so long a space were now become a hell to me; and the change was so rapid, the overthrow so complete!

Jane Austen

From *Northanger Abbey* (1818)

Jane Austen, not really considered a gothic author, wrote *Northanger Abbey* as a parody of the gothic writers and readers she had encountered. In this excerpt, her heroine, Catherine, immersed as she is in the gothic, allows her imagination to run wild in the appropriate setting of Northanger Abbey at night.

The night was stormy; the wind had been rising at intervals the whole afternoon; and by the time the party broke up, it blew and rained violently. Catherine, as she crossed the hall, listened to the tempest with sensations of awe; and, when she heard it rage round a corner of the ancient building and close with sudden fury a distant door, felt for the first time that she was really in an Abbey. – Yes, these were characteristic sounds; – they brought to her recollection a countless variety of dreadful situations and horrid scenes, which such buildings had witnessed, and such storms ushered in; and most heartily did she rejoice in the happier circumstances attending her entrance within walls so solemn!–*She* had nothing to dread from midnight assassins or drunken gallants. Henry had certainly been only in jest in what he had told her that morning. In a house so furnished, and so guarded, she could have nothing to explore or to suffer; and might go to her bedroom as securely as if it had been her own chamber at Fullerton. Thus wisely fortifying her mind, as she proceeded up stairs, she was enabled, especially on perceiving that Miss Tilney slept only two doors from her, to enter her room with a tolerably stout heart; and her spirits were immediately assisted by the cheerful blaze of a wood fire. 'How much better is this' said she, as she walked to the fender – 'how much better to find a fire ready lit, than to have to wait shivering in the cold till all the family are in bed, as so many poor girls have been obliged to do, and then to have a faithful old servant frightening one by coming in with a faggot! How glad I am that Northanger is what it is! If it had been like some other places, I do not know that, in such a night as this, I could have answered for my courage: – but now, to be sure, there is nothing to alarm one.'

   She looked round the room. The window curtains seemed in motion. It could be nothing but the violence of the wind penetrating through the divisions of the shutters; and she stepped boldly forward, carelessly humming a tune, to assure herself of its being so, peeped courageously behind each curtain, saw nothing on either low window seat to scare her, and on placing a hand against the shutter, felt the strongest conviction of the wind's force. A glance at the old chest, as she turned away from this examination, was not without its use; she scorned the causeless fears of an idle fancy, and began with a most happy indifference to prepare herself for bed. 'She should take her time; she should not hurry herself; she did not care if she were the last person up in the house. But she would not make up her fire; *that* would seem cowardly, as if she wished for the protection of light after she were in bed.' The fire, therefore, died away, and Catherine, having spent the best part of an hour in her arrangements, was beginning to think of stepping into bed, when, on giving a parting glance round the room, she was struck by the appearance of a high, old fashioned black cabinet, which, though in a situation conspicuous enough, had never caught her notice before. Henry's words, his description of the ebony cabinet which was to escape her observation at first, immediately rushed across her; and though there could be nothing really in it, there was something whimsical, it was certainly a very remarkable coincidence! She took her candle and looked closely at the cabinet. It was not absolutely ebony and gold; but it was Japan, black and yellow Japan of the handsomest kind; and as she held her candle, the yellow had very much the effect of gold. The key was in the door, and she had a strange fancy to look into it; not however with the smallest expectation of finding anything, but it was so very odd, after what Henry had said. In short, she could not sleep till she had examined it. So, placing the candle with great caution on a chair, she seized the key with a very tremulous hand and tried to turn it; but it resisted her utmost strength. Alarmed, but not discouraged, she tried it another way; a bolt flew, and she believed herself successful but how strangely mysterious! – the door was still immoveable. She paused a moment in breathless wonder. The wind roared down the chimney, the rain beat in torrents against the windows, and everything seemed to speak the awfulness of her situation. To retire to bed, however, unsatisfied on such a point, would be vain, since sleep must be impossible with the consciousness of a cabinet so mysteriously closed in her immediate vicinity. Again therefore she applied herself to the key, and after moving it in every possible way for some instants with the determined celerity of hope's last effort, the door suddenly yielded to her hand: her heart leaped with exultation at such a victory, and having thrown open each folding door, the second being secured only by bolts of less wonderful construction than the lock, though in that her eye could not discern any thing unusual, a double range of small drawers appeared in view, with some larger drawers above and below them, and in the centre, a small door, closed also with lock and key, secured in all probability a cavity of importance.

Catherine's heart beat quick, but her courage did not fail her. With a cheek flushed by hope, and an eye straining with curiosity, her fingers grasped the handle of a drawer and drew it forth. It was entirely empty. With less alarm and greater eagerness she seized a second, a third, a fourth; each was equally empty. Not one was left unsearched, and in not one was anything found. Well read in the art of concealing a treasure, the possibility of false linings to the drawers did not escape her, and she felt round each with anxious acuteness in vain. The place in the middle alone remained now unexplored; and though she had 'never from the first had the smallest idea of finding any thing in any part of the cabinet, and was not in the least disappointed at her ill success thus far, it would be foolish not to examine it thoroughly while she was about it.' It was some time however before she could unfasten the door, the same difficulty occurring in the management of this inner lock as of the outer; but at length it did open; and not in vain, as hitherto, was her search; her quick eyes directly fell on a roll of paper pushed back into the further part of the cavity, apparently for concealment, and her feelings at that moment were indescribable. Her heart fluttered, her knees trembled, and her cheeks grew pale. She seized, with an unsteady hand, the precious manuscript, for half a glance sufficed to ascertain written characters; and while she acknowledged with awful sensations this striking exemplificaton of what Henry had foretold, resolved instantly to peruse every line before she attempted to rest.

The dimness of the light her candle emitted made her turn to it with alarm; but there was no danger of its sudden extinction, it had yet some hours to burn; and that she might not have any greater difficulty in distinguishing the writing than what its ancient date might occasion, she hastily snuffed it. Alas! it was snuffed and extinguished in one. A lamp could not have expired with more awful effect. Catherine, for a few moments, was motionless with horror. It was done completely; not a remnant of light in the wick could give hope to the rekindling breath. Darkness impenetrable and immoveable filled the room. A violent gust of wind, rising with sudden fury, added fresh horror to the moment. Catherine trembled from head to foot. In the pause which succeeded, a sound like receding footsteps and the closing of a distant door struck on her affrighted ear. Human nature could support no more. A cold sweat stood on her forehead, the manuscript fell from her hand, and groping her way to the bed, she jumped hastily in, and sought some suspension of agony by creeping far underneath the clothes. To close her eyes in sleep that night, she felt must be entirely out of the question. With a curiosity so justly awakened, and feelings in every way so agitated, repose must be absolutely impossible. The storm too abroad so dreadful! She had not been used to feel alarm from wind, but now every blast seemed fraught with awful intelligence. The manuscript so wonderfully found, so wonderfully accomplishing the morning's prediction, how was it to be accounted for? – What could it contain? – to whom could it relate? – by what means could it have been so long concealed? – and how singularly strange that it should fall to her lot to discover it! Till she had made herself mistress of its contents, however, she could have neither repose nor comfort; and with the sun's first rays she was determined to peruse it. But many were the tedious hours which must yet intervene. She shuddered, tossed about in her bed, and envied every quiet sleeper. The storm still raged, and various were the noises, more terrific even than the wind, which struck at intervals on her startled ear. The very curtains of her bed seemed at one moment in motion, and at another the lock of her door was agitated, as if by the attempt of somebody to enter. Hollow murmurs seemed to creep along the gallery, and more than once her blood was chilled by the sound of distant moans. Hour after hour passed away, and the wearied Catherine had heard three proclaimed by all the clocks in the house, before the tempest subsided, or she unknowingly fell fast asleep.

John Keats

'La Belle Dame sans Merci' (1820)

The poet Robert Graves, in The *White Goddess* (1948) described this poem as representing 'Love, Death … and Poetry all at once'. Again, beauty is both seductive and deceptive in true gothic style.

La Belle Dame sans Merci

O what can ail thee, knight-at-arms,
  Alone and palely loitering?
The sedge has withered from the lake,
  And no birds sing.

O what can ail thee, knight-at-arms,
  So haggard and so woe-begone?
The squirrel's granary is full,
  And the harvest's done.

I see a lily on thy brow
  With anguish moist and fever dew,
And on thy cheeks a fading rose
  Fast withereth too.

I met a lady in the meads,
  —Full beautiful-a faery's child,
Her hair was long, her foot was light,
  And her eyes were wild.

I made a garland for her head,
  And bracelets too, and fragrant zone;
She looked at me as she did love,
  And made sweet moan.

I set her on my pacing steed,
  And nothing else saw all day long,
For sidelong would she bend, and sing
  A faery's song.

She found me roots of relish sweet,
  And honey wild, and manna dew,
And sure in language strange she said—
  'I love thee true.'

She took me to her elfin grot,
  And there she wept, and sighed full sore,
And there I shut her wild wild eyes
  With kisses four.

And there she lullèd me asleep,
  And there I dreamed—ah, woe betide!
The latest dream I ever dream'd
  On the cold hill's side.

I saw pale kings and princes too,
  Pale warriors, death-pale were they all;
They cried—'La Belle Dame sans Merci
  Hath thee in thrall!'

I saw their starved lips in the gloam,
  With horrid warning gapèd wide,
And I awoke and found me here,
  On the cold hill's side.

And this is why I sojourn here,
  Alone and palely loitering,
Though the sedge is withered from the lake,
  And no birds sing.

Edgar Allan Poe

'The Raven' (1845)

A characteristic example of Poe's imaginative use of gothic imagery: apparently
bleak, doom-laden, enigmatic, dream-like and yet at the same time strangely
appealing. The first-person narrative style gives the poem a rather more intimate
feel than the previous examples of gothic-inspired verse.

The Raven

Once upon a midnight dreary, while I pondered, weak and weary,
Over many a quaint and curious volume of forgotten lore—While I
nodded, nearly napping, suddenly there came a tapping,
As of someone gently rapping, rapping at my chamber door. ''Tis some
visitor,' I muttered, 'tapping at my chamber door—
                    Only this and nothing more.'

Ah, distinctly I remember it was in the bleak December;
And each separate dying ember wrought its ghost upon the floor.
Eagerly I wished the morrow; vainly I had sought to borrow From my
books surcease of sorrow—sorrow for the lost Lenore—
For the rare and radiant maiden whom the angels name Lenore—
                    Nameless *here* for evermore.

And the silken, sad, uncertain rustling of each purple curtain
Thrilled me—filled me with fantastic terrors never felt before;
So that now, to still the beating of my heart, I stood repeating,
''Tis some visitor entreating entrance at my chamber door—
Some late visitor entreating entrance at my chamber door—
                    This it is and nothing more.'

Presently my soul grew stronger; hesitating then no longer, 'Sir,' said I,
'or Madam, truly your forgiveness I implore;
But the fact is I was napping, and so gently you came rapping,
And so faintly you came tapping, tapping at my chamber door,
That I scarce was sure I heard you'—here I opened wide the door-
                    Darkness there and nothing more.

Deep into that darkness peering, long I stood there wondering, fearing,
Doubting, dreaming dreams no mortal ever dared to dream before;
But the silence was unbroken, and the stillness gave no token,
And the only word there spoken was the whispered word, 'Lenore?'
This I whispered, and an echo murmured back the word, 'Lenore!'
                    Merely this and nothing more.

Back into the chamber turning, all my soul within me burning,
Soon again I heard a tapping somewhat louder than before.
'Surely,' said I, 'surely that is something at my window lattice;
Let me see, then, what thereat is, and this mystery explore—
Let my heart be still a moment and this mystery explore—
                    'Tis the wind and nothing more!'

Open here I flung the shutter, when, with many a flirt and flutter,
In there stepped a stately Raven of the saintly days of yore;
Not the least obeisance made he; not a minute stopped or stayed he;
But, with mien of lord or lady, perched above my chamber door—
Perched upon a bust of Pallas just above my chamber door—
                    Perched, and sat, and nothing more.

Then this ebony bird beguiling my sad fancy into smiling,
By the grave and stern decorum of the countenance it wore,
'Though thy crest be shorn and shaven, thou,' I said, 'art sure no craven,
Ghastly grim and ancient Raven wandering from the Nightly shore—
Tell me what thy lordly name is on the Night's Plutonian shore!'
                    Quoth the Raven, 'Nevermore.'

Much I marvelled this ungainly fowl to hear discourse so plainly,
Though its answer little meaning—little relevancy bore;
For we cannot help agreeing that no living human being
Ever yet was blessed with seeing bird above his chamber door—
Bird or beast upon the sculptured bust above his chamber door,
                    With such name as 'Nevermore.'

But the Raven, sitting lonely on the placid bust, spoke only
That one word, as if his soul in that one word he did outpour.
Nothing farther then he uttered—not a feather then he fluttered—
Till I scarcely more than muttered, 'Other friends have flown before—
On the morrow *he* will leave me, as my Hopes have flown before.'
                    Then the bird said, 'Nevermore.'

Startled at the stillness broken by reply so aptly spoken,
'Doubtless,' said I, 'what it utters is its only stock and store
Caught from some unhappy master whom unmerciful Disaster
Followed fast and followed faster till his songs one burden bore—
Till the dirges of his Hope that melancholy burden bore—
                    Of "Never—nevermore."'

But the Raven still beguiling my sad fancy into smiling,
Straight I wheeled a cushioned seat in front of bird and bust and door;
Then, upon the velvet sinking, I betook myself to linking
Fancy unto fancy, thinking what this ominous bird of yore—
What this grim, ungainly, ghastly, gaunt, and ominous bird of yore
                    Meant in croaking 'Nevermore.'

This I sat engaged in guessing, but no syllable expressing
To the fowl whose fiery eyes now burned into my bosom's core;
This and more I sat divining, with my head at ease reclining
On the cushion's velvet lining that the lamplight gloated o'er,
But whose velvet-violet lining with the lamplight gloating o'er,
                    She shall press, ah, nevermore!

Then, methought, the air grew denser, perfumed from an unseen censer
Swung by seraphim whose footfalls tinkled on the tufted floor.
'Wretch,' I cried, 'thy God hath lent thee-by these angels he hath sent thee
Respite—respite and nepenthe from thy memories of Lenore;
Quaff, oh quaff this kind nepenthe and forget this lost Lenore!'
                    Quoth the Raven, 'Nevermore.'

'Prophet!' said I, 'thing of evil!—prophet still, if bird or devil!—
Whether Tempter sent, or whether tempest tossed thee here ashore,
Desolate yet all undaunted, on this desert land enchanted—
On this home by Horror haunted-tell me truly, I implore—.
Is there—*is* there balm in Gilead?—tell me—tell me, I implore!'
                    Quoth the Raven, 'Nevermore.'

'Prophet!' said I, 'thing of evil!—prophet still, if bird or devil!
By that Heaven that bends above us-by that God we both adore—
Tell this soul with sorrow laden if, within the distant Aidenn,
It shall clasp a sainted maiden whom the angels name Lenore—
Clasp a rare and radiant maiden whom the angels name Lenore.'
                    Quoth the Raven, 'Nevermore.'

'Be that word our sign of parting, bird or fiend!' I shrieked, upstarting—
'Get thee back into the tempest and the Night's Plutonian shore!
Leave no black plume as a token of that lie thy soul hath spoken!
Leave my loneliness unbroken!—quit the bust above my door!
Take thy beak from out my heart, and take thy form from off my door!'
                    Quoth the Raven, 'Nevermore.'

And the Raven, never flitting, still is sitting, *still* is sitting
On the pallid bust of Pallas just above my chamber door;
And his eyes have all the seeming of a demon's that is dreaming,
And the lamplight o'er him streaming throws his shadow on the floor;
And my soul from out that shadow that lies floating on the floor
                    Shall be lifted—nevermore!

Emily Brontë

From *Wuthering Heights* (1847)

Emily Brontë's complex, darkly atmospheric novel of human passion displays many gothic characteristics. In this extract, Lockwood, the chief narrator and representative of 'conventional normality', finds himself alone at night for the first time in Heathcliff's sinister home, Wuthering Heights.

This time, I remembered I was lying in the oak closet, and I heard distinctly the gusty wind, and the driving of the snow; I heard, also, the fir-bough repeat its teasing sound, and ascribed it to the right cause: but it annoyed me so much, that I resolved to silence it, if possible; and, I thought, I rose and endeavoured to unhasp the casement. The hook was soldered into the staple: a circumstance observed by me when awake, but forgotten. "I must stop it, nevertheless!" I muttered, knocking my knuckles through the glass, and stretching an arm out to seize the importunate branch; instead of which, my fingers closed on the fingers of a little, ice-cold hand! The intense horror of nightmare came over me: I tried to draw back my arm, but the hand clung to it, and a most melancholy voice sobbed, "Let me in – let me in!" "Who are you?" I asked, struggling, meanwhile, to disengage myself. "Catherine Linton," it replied, shiveringly (why did I think of *Linton*? I had read *Earnshaw* twenty times for Linton); "I'm come home: I'd lost my way on the moor!" As it spoke, I discerned, obscurely, a child's face looking through the window. Terror made me cruel; and, finding it useless to attempt shaking the creature off, I pulled its wrist on to the broken pane, and rubbed it to and fro till the blood ran down and soaked the bedclothes: still it wailed, "Let me in!" and maintained its tenacious gripe, almost maddening me with fear. "How can I?" I said at length. "Let me go, if you want me to let you in! " The fingers relaxed. I snatched mine through the hole, hurriedly piled the books up in a pyramid against it, and stopped my ears to exclude the lamentable prayer. I seemed to keep them closed above a quarter of an hour; yet, the instant I listened again, there was the doleful cry moaning on! "Begone!" I shouted. "I'll never let you in, not if you beg for twenty years." "It is twenty years," mourned the voice: "twenty years. I've been a waif for twenty years!" Thereat began a feeble scratching outside, and the pile of books moved as if thrust forward. I tried to jump up, but could not stir a limb; and so yelled aloud, in a frenzy of fright. To my confusion, I discovered the yell was not ideal: hasty footsteps approached my chamber door; somebody pushed it open, with a vigorous hand, and a light glimmered through the squares at the top of the bed. I sat shuddering yet, and wiping the perspiration from my forehead: the intruder appeared to hesitate, and muttered to himself. At last, he said in a half-whisper, plainly not expecting an answer "Is any one here?" I considered it best to confess my presence, for I knew Heathcliff's accents, and feared he might search further if I kept quiet. With this intention, I turned and opened the panels. I shall not soon forget the effect my action produced.

Heathcliff stood near the entrance, in his shirt and trousers: with a candle dripping over his fingers, and his face as white as the wall behind him. The first creak of the oak startled him like an electric shock! the light leaped from his hold to a distance of some feet, and his agitation was so extreme that he could hardly pick it up.

"It is only your guest, sir," I called out, desirous to spare him the humiliation of exposing his cowardice further. "I had the misfortune to scream in my sleep, owing to a frightful nightmare. I'm sorry I disturbed you."

"Oh, God confound you, Mr. Lockwood! I wish you were at the – " commenced my host, setting the candle on a chair, because he found it impossible to hold it steady. "And who showed you up to this room?" he continued, crushing his nails into the palms, and grinding his teeth to subdue the maxillary convulsions. "Who was it? I've a good mind to turn them out of the house this moment!"

"It was your servant, Zillah," I replied, flinging myself on to the floor, and rapidly resuming my garments. "I should not care if you did, Mr. Heathcliff; she richly deserves it. I suppose that she wanted to get another proof that the place was haunted, at my expense. Well, it is – swarming with ghosts and goblins! You have reason in shutting it up, I assure you. No one will thank you for a doze in such a den!"

"What do you mean?" asked Heathcliff, "and what are you doing? Lie down and finish out the night, since you are here; but, for Heaven's sake! don't repeat that horrid noise; nothing could excuse it, unless you were having your throat cut!"

Robert Louis Stevenson

From *Dr Jekyll and Mr Hyde* (1886)
A seminal story in the development of the gothic, *Dr Jekyll and Mr Hyde* combines horror with astute psychological insight. In this passage, the inventive doctor (an enquiring scientist, not unlike Frankenstein), narrating the tale, encounters for the first time his evil *doppelganger*, or double, Mr Hyde.

I hesitated long before I put this theory to the test of practice. I knew well that I risked death; for any drug that so potently controlled and shook the very fortress of identity, might by the least scruple of an overdose or at the least inopportunity in the moment of exhibition, utterly blot out that immaterial tabernacle which I looked to it to change. But the temptation of a discovery so singular and profound, at last overcame the suggestions of alarm. I had long since prepared my tincture; I purchased at once, from a firm of wholesale chemists, a large quantity of a particular salt which I knew, from my experiments, to be the last ingredient required; and late one accursed night, I compounded the elements, watched them boil and smoke together in the glass, and when the ebullition had subsided, with a strong glow of courage, drank off the potion.

The most racking pangs succeeded: a grinding in the bones, deadly nausea, and a horror of the spirit that cannot be exceeded at the hour of birth or death. Then these agonies began swiftly to subside, and I came to myself as if out of a great sickness. There was something strange in my sensations, something indescribably new and, from its very novelty, incredibly sweet. I felt younger, lighter, happier in body; within I was conscious of a heady recklessness, a current of disordered sensual images running like a mill race in my fancy, a solution of the bonds of obligation, an unknown but not an innocent freedom of the soul. I knew myself, at the first breath of this new life, to be more wicked, tenfold more wicked, sold a slave to my original evil; and the thought, in that moment, braced and delighted me like wine. I stretched out my hands, exulting in the freshness of these sensations; and in the act, I was suddenly aware that I had lost in stature.

There was no mirror, at that date, in my room; that which stands beside me as I write, was brought there later on and for the very purpose of these transformations. The night, however, was far gone into the morning—the morning, black as it was, was nearly ripe for the conception of the day—the inmates of my house were locked in the most rigorous hours of slumber; and I determined, flushed as I was with hope and triumph, to venture in my new shape as far as to my bedroom. I crossed the yard, wherein the constellations looked down upon me, I could have thought, with wonder, the first creature of that sort that their unsleeping vigilance had yet disclosed to them; I stole through the corridors, a stranger in my own house; and coming to my room, I saw for the first time the appearance of Edward Hyde.

I must here speak by theory alone, saying not that which I know, but that which I suppose to be most probable. The evil side of my nature, to which I had now transferred the stamping efficacy, was less robust and less developed than the good which I had just deposed. Again, in the course of my life, which had been, after all, nine tenths a life of effort, virtue and control, it had been much less exercised and much less exhausted. And hence, as I think, it came about that Edward Hyde was so much smaller, slighter and younger than Henry Jekyll. Even as good shone upon the countenance of the one, evil was written broadly and plainly on the face of the other. Evil besides (which I must still believe to be the lethal side of man) had left on that body an imprint of deformity and decay. And yet when I looked upon that ugly idol in the glass, I was conscious of no repugnance, rather of a leap of welcome. This, too, was myself. It seemed natural and human. In my eyes it bore a livelier image of the spirit, it seemed more express and single, than the imperfect and divided countenance, I had been hitherto accustomed to call mine. And in so far I was doubtless right. I have observed that when I wore the semblance of Edward Hyde, none could come near to me at first without a visible misgiving of the flesh. This, as I take it, was because all human beings, as we meet them, are commingled out of good and evil: and Edward Hyde, alone in the ranks of mankind, was pure evil.

I lingered but a moment at the mirror: the second and conclusive experiment had yet to be attempted; it yet remained to be seen if I had lost my identity beyond redemption and must flee before daylight from a house that was no longer mine; and hurrying back to my cabinet, I once more prepared and drank the cup, once more suffered the pangs of dissolution, and came to myself once more with the character, the stature and the face of Henry Jekyll.

That night I had come to the fatal cross roads. Had I approached my discovery in a more noble spirit, had I risked the experiment while under the empire of generous or pious aspirations, all must have been otherwise, and from these agonies of death and birth, I had come forth an angel instead of a fiend. The drug had no discriminating action; it was neither diabolical nor divine; it but shook the doors of the prisonhouse of my disposition; and like the captives of Philippi, that which stood within ran forth. At that time my virtue slumbered; my evil, kept awake by ambition, was alert and swift to seize the occasion; and the thing that was projected was Edward Hyde. Hence, although I had now two characters as well as two appearances, one was wholly evil, and the other was still the old Henry Jekyll, that incongruous compound of whose reformation and improvement I had already learned to despair. The movement was thus wholly toward the worse.

Bram Stoker

From *Dracula* (1897)

Every bit as famous as *Frankenstein*, and just as frequently filmed, *Dracula*
represents the gothic horror story *par excellence*. This passage appears quite near
the novel's opening, and shows the hapless Jonathan Harker, seemingly alone in
Castle Dracula, meeting first the evilly seductive women of the house, and then the
Count himself.

I suppose I must have fallen asleep; I hope so, but I fear, for all that
followed was startlingly real – so real that now, sitting here in the
broad, full sunlight of the morning, I cannot in the least believe that it
was all sleep.

I was not alone. The room was the same, unchanged in any way
since I came into it; I could see along the floor, in the brilliant
moonlight, my own footsteps marked where I had disturbed the long
accumulation of dust. In the moonlight opposite me were three
young women, ladies by their dress and manner. I thought at the time
that I must be dreaming when I saw them, for, though the moonlight
was behind them, they threw no shadow on the floor. They came
close to me and looked at me for some time, and then whispered
together. Two were dark, and had high aquiline noses like the Count,
and great dark, piercing eyes, that seemed to be almost red when
contrasted with the pale yellow moon. The other was fair, as fair as
can be, with great, wavy masses of golden hair and eyes like pale
sapphires. I seemed somehow to know her face, and to know it in
connection with some dreamy fear, but I could not recollect at the
moment how or where. All three had brilliant white teeth, that shone
like pearls against the ruby of their voluptuous lips. There was
something about them that made me uneasy, some longing and at
the same time some deadly fear. I felt in my heart a wicked, burning
desire that they would kiss me with those red lips. It is not good to
note this down, lest some day it should meet Mina's eyes and cause
her pain, but it is the truth. They whispered together, and then they
all three laughed – such a silvery, musical laugh, but as hard as though
the sound could never have come through the softness of human lips.
It was like the intolerable, tingling sweetness of water-glasses when
played on by a cunning hand. The fair girl shook her head
coquettishly, and the other two urged her on. One said:

'Go on! You are first, and we shall follow; yours is the right to
begin.' The other added.

'He is young and strong; there are kisses for us all.' I lay quiet,
looking out under my eyelashes in an agony of delightful anticipation.

The fair girl advanced and bent over me till I could feel the movement of her breath upon me. Sweet it was in one sense, honey-sweet, and sent the same tingling through the nerves as her voice, but with a bitter underlying the sweet, a bitter offensiveness, as one smells in blood.

I was afraid to raise my eyelids, but looked out and saw perfectly under the lashes. The fair girl went on her knees, and bent over me, fairly gloating. There was a deliberate voluptuousness which was both thrilling and repulsive, and as she arched her neck she actually licked her lips like an animal, till I could see in the moonlight the moisture shining on the scarlet lips and on the red tongue as it lapped the white, sharp teeth. Lower and lower went her head as the lips went below the range of my mouth and chin and seemed about to fasten on my throat. Then she paused and I could hear the churning sound of her tongue as it licked her teeth and lips, and could feel the hot breath on my neck. Then the skin of my throat began to tingle as one's flesh does when the hand that is to tickle it approaches nearer – nearer. I could feel the soft, shivering touch of the lips on the supersensitive skin of my throat, and the hard dents of two sharp teeth, just touching and pausing there. I closed my eyes in a languorous ecstasy and waited – waited with beating heart.

But at that instant another sensation swept through me as quick as lightning. I was conscious of the presence of the Count, and of his being as if lapped in a storm of fury. As my eyes opened involuntarily I saw his strong hand grasp the slender neck of the fair woman and with giant's power draw it back, the blue eyes transformed with fury, the white teeth champing with rage, and the fair cheeks blazing red with passion. But the Count! Never did I imagine such wrath and fury even in the demons of the pit. His eyes were positively blazing. The red light in them was lurid, as if the flames of hell-fire blazed behind them. His face was deathly pale, and the lines of it were hard like drawn wires; the thick eyebrows that met over the nose now seemed like a heaving bar of white-hot metal. With a fierce sweep of his arm, he hurled the woman from him, and then motioned to the others, as though he were beating them back; it was the same imperious gesture that I had seen used to the wolves. In a voice which, though low and almost a whisper, seemed to cut through the air and then ring round the room, he exclaimed:

'How dare you touch him, any of you? How dare you cast eyes on him when I had forbidden it? Back, I tell you all! This man belongs to me! Beware how you meddle with him, or you'll have to deal with me.' The fair girl, with a laugh of ribald coquetry, turned to answer him:

'You yourself never loved; you never love!' On this the other women joined, and such a mirthless, hard, soulless laughter rang through the room that it almost made me faint to hear; it seemed like the pleasure of fiends. The Count turned, after looking at my face attentively, and said in a soft whisper:

'Yes, I too can love; you yourselves can tell it from the past. Is it not so? Well, now I promise you that when I am done with him, you shall kiss him at your will. Now go! go! I must awaken him, for there is work to be done.'

'Are we to have nothing tonight?' said one of them, with a low laugh, as she pointed to the bag which he had thrown upon the floor, and which moved as though there were some living thing within it. For answer he nodded his head. One of the women jumped forward and opened it. If my ears did not deceive me there was a gasp and a low wail, as of a half-smothered child. The women closed round, whilst I was aghast with horror but as I looked they disappeared, and with them the dreadful bag. There was no door near them, and they could not have passed me without my noticing. They simply seemed to fade into the rays of the moonlight and pass out through the window, for I could see outside the dim, shadowy forms for a moment before they entirely faded away.

Then the horror overcame me, and I sank down unconscious.

Susan Hill

From *The Woman in Black* (1983)

Susan Hill has herself called this short novel 'a ghost story', and 'a story about evil', and on both counts it seems firmly in the gothic tradition. Here, the narrator, alone in the eerie Eel Marsh House, is awakened by strange sounds. The nature of the evil has yet to be revealed to him, or to the reader.

... Then from somewhere, out of that howling darkness, a cry came to my ears, catapulting me back into the present and banishing all tranquillity.

I listened hard. Nothing. The tumult of the wind, like a banshee, and the banging and rattling of the window in its old, ill-fitting frame. Then yes, again, a cry, that familiar cry of desperation and anguish, a cry for help from a child somewhere out on the marsh.

There was no child. I knew that. How could there be? Yet how could I lie here and ignore even the crying of some long-dead ghost?

'Rest in peace,' I thought, but this poor one did not, could not.

After a few moments I got up. I would go down into the kitchen and make myself a drink, stir up the fire a little and sit beside it trying, trying to shut out that calling voice for which I could do nothing, and no one had been able to do anything for … how many years?

As I went out onto the landing, Spider the dog following me at once, two things happened together. I had the impression of someone who had just that very second before gone past me on their way from the top of the stairs to one of the other rooms, and, as a tremendous blast of wind hit the house so that it all but seemed to rock at the impact, the lights went out. I had not bothered to pick up my torch from the bedside table and now I stood in the pitch blackness, unsure for a moment of my bearings.

And the person who had gone by, and who was now in this house with me? I had seen no one, felt nothing. There had been no movement, no brush of a sleeve against mine, no disturbance of the air, I had not even heard a footstep. I had simply the absolutely certain sense of someone just having passed close to me and gone away down the corridor. Down the short narrow corridor that led to the nursery whose door had been so firmly locked and then, inexplicably, opened.

For a moment, I actually began to conjecture that there was indeed someone – another human being – living here in this house, a person who hid themselves away in that mysterious nursery and came out at night to fetch food and drink and to take the air. Perhaps it was the woman in black? Had Mrs Drablow harboured some reclusive old sister or retainer, had she left behind her a mad friend that no one had known about? My brain span all manner of wild, incoherent fantasies as I tried desperately to provide a rational explanation for the presence I had been so aware of. But then they ceased. There was no living occupant of Eel Marsh House other than myself and Samuel Daily's dog. Whatever was about, whoever I had seen, and heard rocking, and who had passed me by just now, whoever had opened the locked door was not 'real'. No. But what *was* 'real'? At that moment I began to doubt my own reality.

The first thing I must have was a light and I groped my way back across to my bed, reached over it and got my hand to the torch at last, took a step back, stumbled over the dog who was at my heels and dropped the torch. It went spinning away across the floor and fell somewhere by the window with a crash and the faint sound of breaking glass. I cursed but managed, by crawling about on my hands and knees, to find it again and to press the switch. No light came on. The torch had broken.

For a moment I was as near to weeping tears of despair and fear, frustration and tension, as I had ever been since my childhood. But instead of crying I drummed my fists upon the floorboards, in a burst of violent rage, until they throbbed.

It was Spider who brought me to my sense by scratching a little at my arm and then by licking the hand I stretched out to her. We sat on the floor together and I hugged her warm body to me, glad of her, thoroughly ashamed of myself, calmer and relieved, while the wind boomed and roared without, and again and again I heard that child's terrible cry borne on the gusts towards me.

I would not sleep again, of that I was sure, but nor did I dare to go down the stairs in that utter darkness, surrounded by the noise of the storm, unnerved by the awareness I had had of the presence of that other one. My torch was broken. I must have a candle, some light, however faint and frail, to keep me company. There was a candle near at hand. I had seen it earlier, on the table beside the small bed in the nursery.

For a very long time, I could not summon up sufficient courage to grope my way along that short passage to the room which I realised was somehow both the focus and the source of all the strange happenings in the house. I was lost to everything but my own fears, incapable of decisive, coherent thought, let alone movement. But gradually I discovered for myself the truth of the axiom that a man cannot remain indefinitely in a state of active terror. Either the emotion will increase until, at the prompting of more and more dreadful events and apprehensions, he is so overcome by it that he runs away or goes mad; or he will become by slow degrees less agitated and more in possession of himself.

Critical approaches

- How may the views of literary critics help the reader increase his or her understanding of gothic literature?

- What should be the principal purpose of literary criticism, especially as it relates to the gothic tradition?

- What do the main schools of literary criticism – the Marxist, Freudian and feminist approaches, for example – have to say about the gothic?

The nature of literary criticism

The reasoned opinions of others, whether professional critics, teachers or fellow students, can be of immense value in enabling the reader to come to terms with the gothic in context, deciding for himself or herself what views to take and judgements to make. This is why the text of this book has been liberally sprinkled with quotations from a range of writers about the gothic. These opinions and others, however, are no substitute for developing one's own literary acumen, and the critical approaches encountered in this section should be seen in this positive context. It is important to guard against the view that criticism is necessarily arid or parasitical, in contrast to the red hot fires of actual creativity. W.B. Yeats (1865–1939) issued a poetic warning about criticism, particularly apposite to the gothic, in his poem 'The Scholars' (1919):

> Bald heads forgetful of their sins,
> Old, learned, respectable bald heads
> Edit and annotate the lines
> That young men, tossing in their beds,
> Rhymed out in love's despair
> To flatter beauty's ignorant ear.

More positively, perhaps, the poet and critic W.H. Auden (1907–1973) listed six uses of literary criticism in his 'Reading' in *The Dyer's Hand and Other Essays* (1963). He desired that literary critics:

1. introduce me to authors or works of which I was hitherto unaware
2. convince me that I have undervalued an author or a work because I had not read them carefully enough

3 show me relations between works of different ages and cultures which I could never have seen for myself because I do not know enough and never shall
4 give a 'reading' of a work which increases my understanding of it
5 throw light upon the process of artistic 'Making'
6 throw light upon the relation of art to life, to science, economics, ethics, religion, etc.

This seems an excellent starting point for a consideration of a range of critical approaches to the gothic. It also, perhaps, gives a convincing rationale for the whole of this book.

Historical survey of critical approaches to the gothic

A number of critical evaluations both of the gothic in general, and of particular writers and texts have been included in Parts 1 and 2. These references and quotations have presented a range of opinions, from the damning of 'sensationalism' to the praise of emotional insights, and have spanned nearly three centuries. Historically, the gothic – insofar as it was recognised as something distinctive at all – tended to receive a bad press, for a number of reasons, many of which have already been mentioned. However, this lowly critical position must be seen in the context of the tremendous popularity of gothic texts amongst a rapidly increasing reading public. As Marilyn Butler points out, 'The gothic taste is not so much aberrant as an extreme instance of a development characteristic of the period: art openly designed for an expanded public.' (from *Romantics, Rebels and Reactionaries: English Literature and its Background, 1760–1830*, 1981) The whole issue gives rise to a question still relevant today: what is the relationship between 'critical judgement' and general mass popularity? Does the one influence the other, or, as was frequently the case with the gothic, are they likely to be at loggerheads?

To summarise some of the contemporary criticisms made of the gothic at its height:

- The gothic was seen as pandering to the very basest emotions, such as fear and lust, and could lead to virtual addiction, a hopeless craving for more of the same.

- Many texts were regarded at worst as sacrilegious, or at best lacking positive reinforcement of Christian piety and the appropriate ethical standards.

- By emphasising emotional adventures, some critics felt that the gothic could well lead young readers, especially females, to mistakenly expect that level of excitement in real life. As a corollary, such readers, realising eventually and perhaps painfully that real life was less exciting, might then become lethargic and apathetic.

- In an era of revolutionary upheaval some commentators regarded the gothic as politically and socially subversive.

Base addiction to the gothic

Coleridge, vividly exemplifying the first of these positions in his review of *The Monk* (in *The Critical Review*, 1797), proclaimed it to be 'a romance, which if a parent saw in the hands of a son or daughter, he might reasonably turn pale'. An anonymous reviewer of the same novel, in *The British Critic*, declared: 'Lust, murder, incest, and every atrocity that can disgrace human nature, brought together, without the apology of probability, or even possibility, for their introduction.' An unsigned article in the *Scots Magazine* of June 1797, with its stress on what the writer saw as gothic addictiveness, provides a further pertinent example; the modern reader may be struck by the similarity in style between this 18th century piece and some warnings about drug dependency two centuries on:

> Hence the perusal of one romance leads, with much more frequency than is the case with works of other kinds, to the speedy perusal of another. Thus, a habit is formed, a habit at first, perhaps, of limited indulgence, but a habit that is continually found more formidable and more encroaching. The appetite becomes too keen to be denied; and, in proportion as it is more urgent, grows less nice and select in its fare. What would formerly have given offence, now gives none. The palate is vitiated or made dull.

It is relatively easy to mock this sort of attitude, especially with the benefit of hindsight and changing moral standards, but does it in fact express a justifiable warning? If the subject matter referred to were, say, child pornography on the internet, would – or should – attitudes today be any different?

Sacrilegious gothic

The religious context of contemporary reactions to the gothic has been considered in some detail in Part 1 (see pages 18–22). In particular, Matthew Lewis's *The Monk* attracted some of the fiercest denunciations from the devout. For example, Coleridge, in the same review quoted above, reserved his strongest language to denounce *The Monk* for what he saw as its wilful perversion of Christianity:

> We believe it not absolutely impossible that a mind may be so deeply depraved by the habit of reading lewd and voluptuous tales, as to use even the Bible in conjuring up the spirit of uncleanness. The most innocent expressions might become the first link in the chain of association, when a man's soul had been so poisoned; and we believe

it not absolutely impossible that he might extract pollution from the word of purity, and, in a literal sense, *turn the grace of God into wantonness.*

▶ What do you understand by the phrase 'to use even the Bible in conjuring up the spirit of uncleanness'? What defence do you think Matthew Lewis, author of *The Monk*, might have made against such vehement criticism?

Too much gothic excitement?

This is quite a subtle criticism. Its basis, essentially, is the view that too much excitement is bad for people, particularly the young and the female. This is not because of any intrinsically negative qualities in excitement itself, but rather *because* it is attractive – rather more attractive than the stable, unquestioning lives which would be the lot of most 18th century readers, especially upper middle class women. The point relates also to that made above on the addictive nature of the gothic: as with any addictive experience, the excitement will not last, and the fall to harsh reality is likely to be all the harder. Or so conventional wisdom had it. It would be at this point that atrophy might set in for the habitual reader of gothic texts: unfulfilled in finding true life gothic romance, yet dissatisfied with the required dull domesticity. As Fred Botting makes clear, this is a fundamentally conservative position:

> Gothic fictions presented different, more exciting worlds in which heroines in particular could encounter not only frightening violence but also adventurous freedom. The artificiality of narratives imagined other worlds and also challenged the forms of nature and reality advocated by 18th century social and domestic ideology.
>
> (from *Gothic: The New Critical Idiom*, 1996)

The political dimension

The last of the critical positions summarised in the list above, the political, is closely related to the previous observation: that the gothic needlessly, and dangerously, disturbs the social and political equilibrium. Some of the complexities of the political context have been examined previously in Part 1: particularly the sense that for every critic finding revolutionary excess under each gothic gravestone, another would find a more conservative message in the warnings about the horrors of an unstable world in turmoil. One writer of the time, Thomas Mathias (1754–1835), made explicit the link between the taste for the gothic and the threat of revolutionary ideas and philosophies. In his *The Pursuits of Literature* (1794–1797), Mathias's views are vitriolically expressed, managing to combine sexism and xenophobia in one short sentence: 'Our *unsexed* female writers now instruct, or confuse, us and themselves in the labyrinths of politics, or turn us wild with Gallic frenzy.' Elsewhere, Mathias himself uses gothic imagery to underline his point, initiating what later became a tradition of conservative political commentary in which gothic sensationalism was used to portray revolutionary excess, especially when foreign:

> When I have read and thought deeply on the accumulated horrors, and on all the gradations of wickedness and misery, through which the modern systematic philosophy of Europe has conducted her illuminated votaries to the confines of political death and mental darkness, my mind for a space feels a convulsion, and suffers the nature of an insurrection.

A contemporary commentator not normally associated with the political dimension, the Marquis de Sade, writing in 1800, nevertheless had interesting insights into the political context of the gothic, seeing it as in part a response to revolutionary violence in France:

> This genre was the inevitable product of the revolutionary shocks with which the whole of Europe resounded. For those who were acquainted with all the ills that are brought upon men by the wicked, the romantic novel [as opposed to the gothic novel] was becoming somewhat difficult to write, and merely monotonous to read: there was nobody left who had not experienced more misfortunes in four or five years than could be depicted in a century by literature's most famous novelists: it was necessary to call upon hell for aid in order to arouse interest, and to find in the land of fantasies what was common knowledge from historical observation of man in this iron age.

The worse the political horrors, according to de Sade, the more sensationalist the literature. The observation ties in with previously noted criticisms of the gothic, centring on the possible dulling of the senses through too much exposure to too much lurid stimulation. De Sade, as a writer intent on shocking his readers and as a prisoner in France during the Revolution, was certainly qualified to pass comment. The point also connects with that made on page 49 in relation to Mervyn Peake's response to different horrors in a 20th century political context. Much modern criticism of the gothic is of a political nature – particularly the Marxist and feminist schools – and these approaches will be considered on pages 105–110.

   With the passing of the late 18th and early 19th century heyday of the gothic, critical opinion, in very general terms, grew more balanced, less declamatory. In part this may have been because times were changing and the appeal of the gothic was becoming less prevalent, less vivid or perceived as less dangerous. There developed also a diversification of schools of critical thought (a process still going on today), so that a range of critical positions had at least to be considered before stating an opinion. The critical insights of Walter Scott (1771–1832) during the early 19th century were crucial in ushering in a re-evaluation of the significance of the gothic, concentrating less on the sensationalist aspects of the genre and more on the developing philosophical dimension in novels such as *Frankenstein* – influenced by, but by no means a slave to, gothic conventions. In his review of that novel, in *Blackwood's Magazine* (1818), Scott wrote that:

> A more philosophical and refined use of the supernatural in works of fiction, is proper to that class in which the laws of nature are represented as altered, not for the purpose of pampering the imagination with wonders, but in order to show the probable effect which the proposed miracles would produce on those who witnessed them. In this case, the pleasure ordinarily derived from the marvellous incidents is secondary to that which we extract from observing how mortals like ourselves would be affected …

In effect, criticism was beginning to follow the direction that the gothic novel was itself taking, at least in its more thoughtful manifestations: using gothic characteristics and conventions to explore deeper levels of psychological insight and meaning.

Survey of contemporary critical approaches to the gothic

In the 20th century critics tended to follow this trend. Many modern critics have noted the swift degeneration of the original gothic impulse after its first flush of success in the 1790s. Consider, for instance, Maggie Kilgour's view, itself expressed through gothic imagery:

> The gothic had quickly turned into a Frankenstein's monster, produced by the grave robbing of literary tradition, in which old plots were dug up, dismembered, then half-heartedly stitched together and mechanically revived in lurid new forms which debauched the reader's taste and wasted the author's genius.
> (from *The Rise of the Gothic Novel*, 1995)

Insofar as any critical consensus on the quality of the gothic has emerged, it seems to have crystallised around the position taken by Scott (amongst others of his time, including Coleridge) noted above: that the gothic is significant not so much in itself but for its undoubted influence on the development of the literary tradition. The influential critic Mario Praz, for example, in his introductory essay to a 1968 edition of three gothic novels (*The Castle of Otranto, Vathek* and *Frankenstein*), has maintained that:

> Although the literary quality of the tales of terror is not very high ... the gothic romance grew into one of the most powerful currents in the general literature of the 19th century. Without exaggeration, the assertion may be made that no form of novel writing has ever been as productive as the novel of terror and wonder.

Praz went on to list some of the writers who had benefited from this influence, including such seminal figures as Balzac, Hawthorne, Baudelaire, Rossetti and Poe. More recently, Davenport-Hines has refined this point of view, observing:

> When gothic imagery provides all the emotions and structure of a work of art – when it is gothic for gothic's sake – it may achieve a brief climax of emotional excess in the reader or spectator; but the climax soon dies, and is seldom memorable. If, however, the gothic imagination is enlisted not as a mechanistic technique but as an aesthetic to help convey other sensations or philosophies, then it may deserve lasting attention, as in the cases of Goya and Sade, of Mary Shelley and perhaps 'Monk' Lewis.
>
> (from Gothic, 1998)

▶ The distinction made here is an important one, but is there a sense that critics like Praz and Davenport-Hines are being too harsh in their judgements of 'pure' gothic texts? From your own reading and reflection, consider the issues involved here and work out your own position.

▶ Are there any contemporary parallels here: writers, artists or musicians whose significance may lie not so much in their own achievements but in their influence on others? If so, what does this judgement say about their own, intrinsic value as creative practitioners?

Although there is now a sometimes bewildering diversity of critical approaches to the gothic, it is possible to delineate certain influential schools of thought. Important examples include Freudian, Marxist and feminist approaches and viewpoints – or permutations of all three. A more detailed examination of each of these approaches follows, with a brief summary of the possible application of each critical model to the novel *Frankenstein*, for comparative purposes.

Freud and his influence

Sigmund Freud has already been mentioned several times in this book, notably in connection with his 1919 essay 'The Uncanny' and as founder of psycho-analysis. Although always insistent on the scientific basis of his work, both theoretical and practical, Freud realised that the significance of art as a key to psychology was huge. He had a particular liking for and interest in art on the fringes of human experience, and this is precisely where the gothic comes in. Subsequent followers and interpreters of Freud have developed his insights into literature in a range of ways, and in relation to a variety of texts and authors. Although some of these interpretative positions may be rather more conflicting than complementary, there are certain characteristics of Freud's thought that have permeated all of them. Chief amongst these is the sense that the fully conscious mind is merely a small part of a person's psychology – like the tip of an iceberg – and that the subconscious is a far more powerful motivator of human emotions and actions. As the iceberg metaphor suggests, however, the subconscious remains largely hidden, revealed only in such phenomena as dreams, abnormal behavioural patterns and extremes of emotional intensity. The last of these may, clearly, include art in its general sense. Unsurprisingly, it may have a particular relevance to the gothic: the preoccupation with dream-like images, extremes of emotional response and shades of darkness make the gothic particularly fertile ground for Freudian investigation. Other aspects of Freudian thought are also especially apt in this context, notably:

- the concentration on infancy as the basis of subsequent psychological development
- the notion that sexuality, repressed or otherwise, lies at the root of human behaviour
- the particular emphasis on the relationship between parents and children, developed through the Oedipus complex
- ideas on the psychologically divided self, especially when the 'id' (the appetite-driven emotional basis of life) is in conflict with the 'ego' (the conscious sense of 'self') or the 'super-ego' (the sense of morality, sometimes construed as the conscience)
- the death-wish as a powerful psychological drive, running counter to the desire to live and survive (Freud's 'pleasure principle'), and based on the continuing attraction of a return to the darkness and security of the womb.

In many ways it is the Oedipus complex which is central to all of these, dealing as it does with the notion of the unrealisable sexual desire of the male infant for his mother and consequent desire to remove – kill, in fact – the father, who of course is already in this enviable position. Clearly, problematic parent-child relationships are frequently featured in gothic texts, although not necessarily limited to the sexual obsessions of small boys.

▶ Consider the elements of Freudian thought outlined above and discuss whether and how they could help to understand gothic texts you have read. If so, how helpful do you think Freudian approaches are in developing a critical appreciation of the gothic?

▶ In this context, reflect on the presentation of sexuality and parent-child relationships in *The Monk*. To what extent does a Freudian analysis help to explain the complex sexuality of Ambrosio himself?

Although interested in art, almost as evidence to substantiate his scientific position, Freud did not really pursue the cultural implications of his work. Indeed, one reading of his work suggests that the only value of art is as scientific evidence of psychological instability – particularly, an inability on the behalf of the artist to come to terms with his or her sexuality. Interestingly, in view of Edmund Burke's study of the sublime (see page 50), some strands of Freudian thought have tended to see virtually all human behaviour – including, and perhaps especially, forms of art – as mere 'sublimations' of sexual instincts. Nevertheless, the basic tenets of his thinking have found their way into popular consciousness during the 20th century. Most people, for example, have some notion of the subconscious mind, regard dreams as open to interpretation, and may use expressions like 'a Freudian slip' to denote the intrusion of the subconscious into everyday speech and behaviour. This very ubiquity of popular Freudianism, however, may make a more subtle appreciation of his insights difficult to achieve, and care needs to be taken here to avoid 'crude' applications.

With regard to Mary Shelley's *Frankenstein*, it is possible to see the appropriateness of Freudian approaches in a number of ways. Psychological interpretations of this novel have tended to focus on notions of the subconscious, or, at a still deeper level, the unconscious. Central to the novel, clearly, is the unleashing of terrifyingly uncontrolled dark forces somehow created by the human mind, yet simultaneously chillingly apart from it. As the story develops the comfortable domesticity of Frankenstein's family is disastrously disrupted through his own activities. Hidden beneath the deceptive calm of civilised people and their apparently civilised composure is dark turmoil, symbolised by 'the workshop of filthy creation' and the resulting Creature himself. In Frankenstein's exhausted delirium following his life-bringing labours he dreams of his betrothed, Elizabeth. The dream, however, is a typically Freudian distortion of reality, at once rooted in that reality and terrifyingly distant from it. Elizabeth is dreamed of, not in her usual homely setting, but instead in Ingolstadt, the site of Frankenstein's experiment:

Delighted and surprised, I embraced her; but as I imprinted the first kiss on her lips, they became livid with the hue of death; her features appeared to change, and I thought that I held the corpse of my dead mother in my arms; a shroud enveloped her form, and I saw the grave-worms crawling in the folds of the flannel.

This is extremely fertile ground for a psycho-analytical exploration of the text, hinting as it does at a dark association of sex with death, and at the incestuous nature of Frankenstein's sexuality. In this instance, the sexuality is inseparable from intense guilt, in a classic Oedipal fashion.

There are of course other psychological dimensions to the novel, and here again Freudian insights may be helpful. Frankenstein's own psyche seems damagingly split from the start, between the conventional, affectionate family man on the one hand, and the narrowly ambitious, secretive and anti-social experimenter with forces dangerously beyond his control on the other. This psychic division, it can be argued, achieves material manifestation in the Creature himself. In a way emphasised by several film versions of the novel, it is possible to see Frankenstein and his nearly-human creation as two halves of the same psychic whole, divided yet inseparable. Both halves realise this with varying degrees of consciousness – the Creature rather more perceptively than Frankenstein. For while the latter spends the novel mis-reading vital signs, the Creature goes so far as to point out the essential unity to his creator. Amidst the appropriately dramatic Alpine scenery, he proclaims to Frankenstein, the tormented tormentor, that the two of them 'are bound by ties only dissoluble by the annihilation of one of us'. The Creature is in effect a distorted reflection of the creator: a *doppelganger* in much the same way as Dr Jekyll and Mr Hyde are one and the same person in Stevenson's later novel. To employ Freud's terminology may be interpretively helpful in this context. It is possible to see Frankenstein as Freud's idea of the 'ego', seeking to control the psychic energy of the 'id', symbolised by the hugely powerful Creature. According to this interpretation, it is precisely the inability (or refusal) of the ego to come to terms with the id which leads to their mutual destruction. And this urge towards mutual destruction seems fuelled by a Freudian death wish ultimately victorious over any last remnants of a pleasure principle. Appropriately, it is only in the final scene of Frankenstein's death and the Creature's sense of his own impending doom that some sort of harmony is, albeit tenuously, possible.

THE GOTHIC TRADITION

Marx and his influence

Marxist approaches to literature emphasise the social context and implications of texts, rather than the Freudian individual psychology of fictional characters and/or their authors. The two approaches are not necessarily mutually exclusive, although in the final analysis they are poles apart philosophically. The essential Freudian message is that the individual's psychology to a large extent determines his or her interaction with the rest of society, whereas for the Marxist it is the social context – the material, objective reality – which largely determines and constrains any individual's psychology. Marxist criticism, which has developed into models of cultural analysis, tends towards one or other of two distinctive, yet overlapping, approaches. On the one hand, historical approaches have sought to root texts and their authors firmly in their social and political contexts, and have arrived at those texts through a study of history, seeing them fundamentally as manifestations of particular historical struggles and values. On the other hand are the more distinctively literary approaches, focusing on the social struggles encapsulated within the texts themselves. The latter tend to ascribe rather greater value to literature, allowing that art may itself have a potentially determining impact on social and political forces as well as initially reflecting them. Marxist criticism has travelled a long way since the early days of crude materialism, whereby art was seen simply as a passive reflection of historical forces, and the philosophical tool used to achieve this greater subtlety is the dialectical method. Through this method it is possible to see any historical phenomenon – including literature – in terms of a struggle between a thesis and its antithesis. In either case, the conflict between the two leads to a new stage of reality, a synthesis. This in its turn becomes part of a new struggle with its own opposite (antithesis) in a fresh process of transformation. Thus history is never static. Applied to the gothic phenomenon, this method sees the writer or artist as symptomatic of opposed social forces; the resulting art may be understood as a synthesis, born of struggle, which – potentially – itself then has an influence on history. And the essential struggle which lies at the base of all history, according to the Marxist viewpoint, is that between social classes as formed by the dominant economic reality.

There have been references throughout this book to the social and political context of gothic literature, including the class struggle symptomatic of the fast-emerging capitalism of the late 18th and early 19th centuries. It should be apparent that the gothic is problematic in terms of its possible political interpretation, both to its contemporaries and to modern critics. The essential point, however, is that the gothic, like all literature, has value in this context. Leon Trotsky (1879–1940), who as commander of the Red Army during the Russian Revolution of 1917 was no stranger to the practical realities of class struggle, vehemently opposed Marxist comrades who espoused a narrow, deterministic conception of literature. Writing of

Dante's *Divine Comedy* (but it could conceivably have been about any literary text) in *Class and Art* (1924), Trotsky had this to say:

> Works of art developed in a medieval Italian city can, we find, affect us too. What does this require? A small thing: it requires that these feelings and moods shall have received such broad, intense, powerful expression as to have raised them above the limitations of the life of those days.

It is in this sense that a literary text may be seen as a synthesis, offering clues not only about its social context, but in itself influential in the subsequent direction of that society's development. It may be that the relationship between master and servant in *The Italian*, for example, betrays contemporary anxieties about rapidly changing class relationships; that de Sade saw gothic tales as symptomatic of revolutionary excess; or that the growth of the literate middle class in the 18th century allowed for the rapid development of the novel and the publishing industry. The Marxist point is that, in one way or another, literature connects dynamically with its social, political and economic contexts.

Marxist preoccupations in the field of literary criticism might include:

- an interest in the means by which texts are produced and distributed, and how these may influence the nature of those texts
- the ways in which a text was read by contemporaries in terms of its perceived social or political 'message' or imagery
- the particular historical point at which the text emerged, with emphasis on the historical stage of the class struggle
- how plot, characters and setting may reflect this class struggle through what is included in the text, or, interestingly, what is left out
- how, in terms of the class struggle, characters may become 'outsider' figures, feeling alienated from their social context – their fellow human beings.

▶ In the light of your reading of gothic texts and about the social context, consider how some of the approaches listed above may apply. Do they in any way aid understanding of the texts?

▶ How might Marxist interpretive models relate to those used by Freudian, psychological criticism? As a focus here, develop any insights already gained into *The Monk* to include references to class relationships.

With regard to Mary Shelley's *Frankenstein*, Marxist critical approaches might read this novel as either a revolutionary or a reactionary text. This approach mirrors a certain ambivalence (noted previously, on pages 28–29) in Mary Shelley's own character. Neither does the process of reflection stop there, for a Marxist critique would extend beyond any contradictions in the text, or in the author's biography, towards an exploration of confusing, class-based currents and counter-currents of that particular time. Put simply: Mary Shelley was born of revolutionary parents and married a revolutionary aristocrat (who spent much of his money on furthering the cause of Irish rebellion); yet she saw enough of the reality of social revolution and disintegration to fear the consequences. Indeed she was to claim in later life that the radicals 'are full of repulsion to me – violent without any sense of Justice'. In this ambivalence she personified the plight of the radical intelligentsia of the time, or perhaps of any time, and her work is all the more pertinent.

Through a revolutionary reading of *Frankenstein*, the Creature may be seen as a symbol of the increasingly organised and revolutionary working class and its radical leaders. Most readers feel ambivalent towards the Creature, veering from sympathy for his plight to horror at his crimes, as Mary Shelley felt towards the potential power of the proletariat, the Marxist term for the working class. In this schematic view of the novel, the proletariat owes its existence, miserable as it may be, to the exploitative needs of the respectable middle class – the Marxists' 'bourgeoisie' – as personified by Frankenstein himself. The intention, clearly, is to control, even enslave – but the Creature breaks free and begins to lead an autonomous life, to the extent of dictating terms to his creator. At this point in the narrative there seems to be a faint, fleeting chance of mutual fulfilment, but this is cruelly dashed by the nature of Frankenstein's fear that the Creature's kind would go on to dominate the world. Embittered, alienated (again to use a Marxist term), the Creature, who remains unnamed and all the more fearful, turns violently against the world. As in the Freudian model of interpretation, the relationship between the two is intense and close, and ultimately mutually destructive.

Feminist approaches

In many ways, feminist criticism has grown out of a creative synthesis of Marxist and Freudian approaches, liberated further by the insights of structuralist and post-structuralist readings of literature which have probed ever deeper into the hidden depths of texts. Feminist criticism has emerged as a school in its own right only during the last quarter of the 20th century; as recently as 1968 Mario Praz (in his introductory essay to three gothic novels) was able to pose the question 'why in the most polite and effeminate of centuries ... should people have begun to feel the horrible fascination of dark forests and lugubrious caverns, and cemeteries and thunderstorms?' and come up with the rather patronising answer: 'just because of its feminine character. In no other century was woman such a dominating figure ...

They had vague inklings of a metaphysical anxiety.' Yet it is possible to argue that feminist approaches to literature began with the writings of Mary Wollstonecraft, Mary Shelley's mother, and continued to influence critics thereafter. Coleridge, for example, made the feminist point that Lewis, in *The Monk*, reduces female characters to either 'trembling innocence', in the case of Antonia, or 'shameless harlotry' (Matilda) and then goes on to exploit both male models of femininity as 'vehicles of the most voluptuous images'. This analysis has been developed more recently by such commentators as Maggie Kilgour, who writes of the relationship, in *The Monk*, between Ambrosio and Matilda:

> Her unfeminine assurance and domination over Ambrosio in fact cause him some uneasiness, as they do not correspond to his ideal of feminine behaviour. ... The distinction between the sexes disturbed by the discovery that Rosario is a woman is reaffirmed by the discovery that the woman who has autonomy, reason, and authority is in reality a demon.
>
> (from *The Rise of the Gothic Novel*, 1995)

Insights such as these have led other critics to agree with Victor Sage that 'The most interesting and important work on the Gothick has been feminist.' (from *The Gothick Novel: A Selection of Critical Essays*, ed. Victor Sage, 1990)

Feminist analysis of the gothic might focus on some of the following concerns:

- the relative silence, or, at the very least, passivity, of female characters in many gothic texts

- the stereotyping of female characters according to male fantasy, as Coleridge observed

- conversely, the relevance of some gothic texts to the real concerns and plight of women

- the appropriation of an essentially female invention, the novel, by male canonical authors, achieved, to some extent, by

- the patronising tone of many reviews, forcing many female authors to publish anonymously

- actual textual revisions made by men of texts written by female authors.

In effect, all the above areas apply to an analysis of *Frankenstein*. Much feminist criticism focuses on Mary Shelley's novel as an exploration of and exposure of the folly of masculine posturing – in the role of the ambitious scientist intent on the domination of nature. As such, the character of Frankenstein echoed contemporary scientific discourse; Mary Shelley seemed uncannily, and prophetically, aware of the dangers inherent in a scientific quest that could so easily sacrifice humane means, perhaps humanity itself, in the thirst for knowledge and power. Humphrey Davy, for example, a pioneering scientist read and admired by both Shelleys, enthused about science enabling 'man' to:

> ... change and modify the beings surrounding him, and by his experiments to interrogate nature with power, not simply as a scholar, passive and seeking only to understand her operations, but rather as a master, active with his own instruments.
>
> (from *A Discourse, Introductory to a Course of Lectures on Chemistry*, 1802)

Striking here is the concept of mastery, and the male principle is conventionally emphasised by the use of gendered pronouns. In the novel, even before Frankenstein begins his story, the 'framing' narrator Walton speaks of his quest for 'the dominion I should acquire and transmit over the elemental foes of our race', thus setting the tone for Frankenstein's own ambitions. Mary Shelley subtly undermines and questions such male assumptions throughout the novel, using the text as a prophecy in the sense that William Blake meant when he wrote of a true prophet not foretelling a pre-determined future, but rather warning 'Thus: if you go on So, the result is So.' (from *Marginalia*, 1798)

Frankenstein in the novel goes a step further: not only does he seek to impose his will on passive and characteristically feminine nature, he actually usurps the maternal role of woman in his quest to create life. But of course he cannot, and the result is a disastrous distortion of female creativity. The women actually featured in the novel are powerless, in this competitively masculine world, to stop him. They speak with subdued voices, or they are virtually silent. Frankenstein's mother scarcely appears at all (except in the nightmarish vision mentioned above). Elizabeth is passive and undemanding (although rather less so in recent film versions), seen almost entirely through the eyes of Frankenstein in what verges on an incestuous relationship. Justine is an even more shadowy figure: a habitual victim eventually sacrificed to the avenging Creature. Agatha is largely silent, lacking any vitality, and Safie's fairy-tale feminine sweetness is almost entirely focused on her lover Felix. Significantly, Frankenstein cannot bring himself to create a female counterpart to his male Creature, and at the last moment destroys all his work towards that end.

Further feminist commentary has noted the wider context of the novel. Mary's husband Percy Shelley, for example, undertook wholesale revisions of the work, replacing, at times, her directness of style with a more 'sophisticated' tone and adding vast quantities of punctuation. One feminist critic, Anne Mellor, has suggested that such revisions 'actually distorted the meaning of the text'. (from *Mary Shelley: Her Life, Her Fiction, Her Monsters*, 1988) When Mary Shelley published the novel, in 1818, she was forced to do so anonymously – and many readers and reviewers were so impressed that they believed it to be the work of a man, probably her husband. She did not attach her own name to the work until 1823, by which time Percy was already, tragically, dead.

▶ Consider further the points made above in relation to the novel Frankenstein. Do you think that they could be usefully applied to other gothic texts? If so, which ones?

Assignments

1 Having been introduced to some of the possible critical approaches to gothic texts, and seen how they may be applied to one key novel, *Frankenstein*, consider how appropriate these approaches may be to other examples. It may be best to focus on one short text, perhaps taken from Part 3: Texts and extracts, and then, working in small groups, apply a particular interpretive model to this text. Aim to construct a carefully reasoned justification of your particular 'reading', and go on to present the various approaches in a structured 'critics' debate' session.

   What are the strengths and weaknesses of the different interpretations?

   How may some models be more apt for certain texts than others?

2 In order more fully to explore the possibilities and validity of different readings of your chosen text(s), try developing particular interpretations for one or more of a range of contexts. These could include:
   • a film director considering ideas for a short film version, adapting and selecting material as appropriate
   • a graphic artist working on illustrations of key moments in the text, to accompany a new edition for a specific audience
   • a documentary maker focusing on the biography of the writer, seeking to integrate the life story with the text itself
   • a writer of an abridged version for a particular readership, working on the selection of what is deemed most significant in the text
   • an historian accumulating evidence, from texts and contexts, in order to come to a fuller understanding of the epoch involved.

3 Returning briefly to W.H. Auden's formulation of what he would expect of
a good literary critic (quoted on pages 95–96), consider carefully which –
if any – of his six points have been met in your own encounters with
literary criticism of the gothic.

It may be especially worthwhile to discuss Auden's fourth point ('Give
a "reading" of a work which increases my understanding of it') and add
the word 'enjoyment'. Has an enhanced critical sense added to your
textual understanding or enjoyment?

In the light of the six requirements, which critical approach, or
synthesis of more than one, is closest to your own views?

5 | How to write about the gothic

In addressing this fundamental concern, 'how to write about the gothic', it is important to realise that there is no single 'best way'. Formulaic approaches to writing are likely to lead to formulaic examples of the writer's craft – the broad field of gothic writing itself perhaps provides plenty of examples. Each writer has to find his or her own way in to the subject, adopting an appropriate and lively style as befits the nature of the gothic itself. Nevertheless, there are useful guidelines and suggestions which may aid the writing process: spontaneous originality by itself would be unlikely to produce effective, well structured written responses and any perceptive insights may well remain hidden in the confusion. This point is especially valid for writing about literature in its various contexts. Examples of what might be termed 'good practice' from the range of critical writing alluded to and quoted in this book have tended to emphasise precisely this sense of literature – the gothic, in this instance – in context. There are some fundamental issues to consider in coming to terms with contextual writing about the gothic:

- a sense of genre: what type of text is this?
- an appreciation of purpose: who wrote the text? for whom? when?
- insights into audience: who reads the text? in what ways may it be read?

It is these questions that now need further examination.

A sense of genre

The starting point here is straightforward enough: the type of text being examined will to a large extent determine its characteristics. Each genre, or type, has its own conventions and likely features; for example, a novel is usually of a certain minimum length, is organised in chapters, and tells some sort of story. Similarly, the characteristics of a poem are likely to include rhythmic structure and concentrated language; those of a play would include an emphasis on dialogue and organisation into acts. These, and many others, clearly, are formal manifestations of genres: dealing with the essential form within which any writer must operate. It is also clear that, in order that literature develops and changes, the forms must change: boundaries be pushed back, 'rules' broken, conventions re-invented. With reference to the gothic, this observation seems particularly apt, as writers borrowed, developed and transcended the formal requirements of genres to transform them. The very word 'transform' implies this sort of change. There have been several examples of this process already featured in this book: consider, for instance, Mary Shelley's use of gothic conventions in her writing of *Frankenstein*, which is fundamentally a philosophical novel. Or Susan Hill working within the tradition of the gothic ghost story in *The Woman in Black* in order, as she has said, to address a 'serious underlying purpose' in showing 'how suffering may warp a human personality'.

As these brief examples demonstrate, it is possible, and desirable, to refine notions of genre beyond the basic sense of whether a text is a novel, play or poem. There are within each of these genres many sub-divisions: a ballad, for example, has quite different formal characteristics from a short lyric poem, and a lengthy novel such as *The Monk* progresses in quite different ways than Poe's story 'The Black Cat'. There are also generic considerations which link texts that superficially appear quite different from one another. In fact, this is true of the nature of the gothic itself: however distinct, gothic plays, poems and prose writing may have more similarities to each other, linked as they are by gothic features, than any one example has to a text outside the gothic. For instance, Poe's poem 'The Raven' is rather closer to *The Monk* in many ways than to virtually any poem not in the gothic idiom, despite the fact that both may be poems. So, in writing about genre in gothic literature, there are several dimensions to bear in mind.

Sometimes, a particular text may be adapted for another genre. There have been several instances of this mentioned already: notably, play and film versions of classics such as *Frankenstein* and *Dracula*. The process of adaptation can usefully illuminate conventions in both the original and the new genres. Take, for example, Susan Hill's *The Woman in Black*, a short novel subsequently adapted for the stage by the playwright Stephen Mallatratt. The focus in this adaptation, as Mallatratt has commented, is 'the way it had worked on my imagination'. The task was to find 'some way of telling the story that would allow my actors to speak Susan's descriptive passages as well as the conversations'. Mallatratt, then, was able to use some of the conventions of modern theatre – the play within a play, featuring an actor discussing the craft of acting – in order to realise his aim. At the same time, there occurs in effect a *subversion* of the genre of a play, in that description rather than conversation drives the plot. In many respects, Mallatratt reverts to a pre-18th century dramatic tradition – within which Shakespeare, for example, was working – whereby the words spoken on stage conjure images in the minds of the audience. For 'if that could happen there'd be little need for things like scenery, or ponies, or dogs; all those things would be there – and real – in the mind of every person in the theatre'. And these insights serve to shed light on the textual characteristics of the original genre – Hill's story – with its intense evocation of atmosphere.

To summarise, then: in writing about gothic texts it is important to be aware of genre considerations and stylistic conventions, including some of these possibilities:

- the basic distinction between genres such as novels, poems and plays

- refinements within these categories, such as ghost stories or ballads, with an awareness of how the generic conventions might influence the writing

- cross-genre dimensions, as exemplified above – either in the sense of common ground between texts ostensibly from different genres, or of adaptations across genres

- the relationship between form and content, and in particular how an author may transcend or subvert a genre's conventions in order to convey his or her message. (See Part 2: Approaching the texts, pages 56–57 for a fuller exploration of these relationships.)

An appreciation of purpose

Here the concern is for author, intended readership, and when the text was written: vitally important contextual considerations. In an attempt to concentrate awareness on all three aspects, here are four brief extracts from gothic texts.

> The Caves and mountains rang with Ambrosio's shrieks. The demon continued to soar aloft, till reaching a dreadful height, he released the sufferer. Headlong fell the monk through the airy waste; the sharp point of a rock received him ...
>
> (from Matthew Lewis *The Monk*)

> And now my wanderings began, which are to cease but with life. I have traversed a vast portion of the earth, and have endured all the hardships which travellers, in deserts and barbarous countries, are wont to meet. How I have lived I hardly know; many times have I stretched my failing limbs upon the sandy plain, and prayed for death. But revenge kept me alive; I dared not die, and leave my adversary in being.
>
> (from Mary Shelley *Frankenstein*)

> It is useless, and the time awfully fails me, to prolong this description; no one has ever suffered such torments, let that suffice; and yet even to these, habit brought – no, not alleviation – but a certain callousness of soul, a certain acquiescence of despair; and my punishment might have gone on for years, but for the last calamity which has now fallen, and which has finally severed me from my own face and nature.
>
> (from Robert Louis Stevenson *Dr Jekyll and Mr Hyde*)

This time, there was no merciful loss of consciousness, I was forced to live through it all, every minute and then every day thereafter for ten long months ... . They asked for my story. I have told it. Enough.

(from Susan Hill *The Woman in Black*)

These extracts span two hundred years of gothic writing; all occur towards the end of novels, and deal with the anguish and sufferings of the central characters – more often than not related in the first person. So there are significant similarities, but there are also, clearly, important differences. If writing comparatively about gothic texts, the focus could be on both aspects: 'compare and contrast', as the stock literature question may instruct. In the context of an appreciation of purpose, responses to these texts could usefully centre on:

- your own reactions to the different pieces, based on a close reading

- the stylistic differences as reflecting the different times they were written in

- the diverse authorial intentions represented here, as discovered through research into their backgrounds

- generic similarities in terms of both style and content, despite the very different times – perhaps introducing a consideration of just how significant historical context may be

- an emphasis on the intended readerships, and how readers' expectations may have altered/stayed the same over the 200 years.

Insights into audience

Ultimately, any effective writing on gothic texts must come to terms with a range of critical appraisals, but must also pursue its own interpretive direction. It is important to remember that, as the writer, you are representing an audience, with views as valid as anyone else's – as long as they are rooted in the texts and contexts. (Useful information may be gained into this aspect from Part 4: Critical approaches.)

For example, if writing about *The Monk*, it helps to be aware of various critical opinions – not simply to impress your reader, but to further refine your own views in relation to others'. You could envisage your writing as a dialogue: both with particular texts, and with the opinions of various other readers. Some of these you may wish to challenge, others may be more agreeable; the point is that no opinion has arrived from nowhere in a critical vacuum, so connections need to be made. There have already been a number of quoted responses to this novel; briefly, here are a few more.

... uncontrollable energy would seem to be the only energy there is in the world of *The Monk*. The artist [referring to Lewis himself], like the monk who seeks liberation from lifeless conventions, is apt to find himself unexpectedly on the side of the flood ...

(from Robert Kiely The Romantic Novel in England, 1972)

... a species of brutality, such as no observation of character can justify, because no good man would willingly suffer them to pass, however transiently, through his own mind ...

(anonymous contemporary review in Critical Review)

... The Monk ... feeds off a 'Catholic' aesthetic, though it takes its morality from its Protestantism. Thus, though the convent's procession, with the glittering carriage, impish devils, and beautiful nuns, is shown to us as an example of Catholic substitution of glamour and wealth for religion, it is also that which Lewis's art thrives on. ... Spectacle – violent, showy, abrupt and glittering – is the dominant aesthetic of this work.

(from Emma McEvoy in the Introduction to
The Monk, 1998)

Though sexual passion and the dangers of repression produce much of the story's force, the book also represents repressive social regimes and the horrific mindless violence of the vengeful mobs that attack reactionary authority.
     The power of the book comes from both individual and collective violence.

(from Richard Davenport-Hines Gothic, 1998)

Bearing in mind these brief appraisals, and other 'readings' already encountered, writing about *The Monk* may well usefully develop along these lines:

- what sorts of 'energy' are featured?
- what is suggested about the relationship between text and author?
- what is the nature of any moral purpose gleaned from this novel?
- how significant is the sense of spectacle?
- what are the social, political, psychological and spiritual implications?
- which other texts may bear useful comparison with *The Monk*?

Part of a writer's skill in effectively presenting a critique of literature, gothic or otherwise, is to weave together a range of approaches, based around the questions posed earlier: 'who reads the text?' and 'in what ways may it be read?' Attitudes towards and opinions of *The Monk* have featured prominently throughout this book, and such views provide a rich sense of context. But every reader, and for that matter every writer, has to discover afresh the impact of the text itself. Good critical writing conveys this sense above all else.

Assignments

General

1 Gothic writing has been attacked as 'a species of brutality'. With reference to at least two gothic texts, discuss whether this indictment has any validity.

2 Consider the relationship between the cinema and the gothic literary tradition. Are the two media – cinematic and textual – complementary or in opposition to each other?

3 In what senses is it appropriate to regard the gothic as essentially a reaction to rationalist conceptions of life? Refer to at least two separate texts.

4 'Four hundred years of excess, horror, evil and ruin'. How might a writer working within the gothic tradition mount a defence against such a view?

5 In what ways is it appropriate to see the gothic as a strongly visual aesthetic force? Consider this question in relation to both texts and visual media such as painting or the cinema.

6 How far does the gothic remain elusive as a literary force, impossible to define or pin down? Might this be seen as a strength or a weakness?

7 In relation to at least two texts, consider the view that the gothic is essentially backward looking: nostalgic, escapist and merely titillating.

8 Discuss the presentation of women in any two gothic texts. Was Coleridge justified (in this case, with regard to *The Monk*) in criticising gothic portrayal of women as either 'shameless harlotry' or 'trembling innocence'?

9 Lord Holland said of Matthew Lewis: 'his mind was vitiated with a mystical, though irreligious, philosophy'. Discuss how far this might be an apt judgement of the spiritual values purveyed by gothic texts.

10 Consider the view that the gothic is important not so much for its own achievements as for its influence on more profound literature of more lasting value.

11 Margaret Drabble defined Romanticism as '... an extreme assertion of the self and the value of individual experience. ... The stylistic keynote ... is intensity, and its watchword is "Imagination".' Consider how far this formulation applies also to the gothic, and what its relationship is with Romanticism.

12 To what extent do you agree that a sense of the horrifically macabre is the defining common denominator of all gothic fiction? Is it possible to disentangle the gothic from horror?

On specific texts

13 How do traditional ballads relate to later texts of the gothic revival? In discussing this question, you could focus on issues of form, on themes, and on the nature of the stories told.

14 Compare the presentation of ambivalent attraction in Keats' 'La Belle Dame sans Merci' and Coleridge's 'Christabel'. Is it significant that in both poems such feelings are focused on central female figures?

15 In the light of what you understand of the psychology of dreams, discuss the impact of Poe's 'The Raven', and the dream sequences from Mary Shelley's *Frankenstein* and Emily Brontë's *Wuthering Heights*. Is intertextual comparison helpful in this context?

16 The critic Elizabeth Napier regarded Walpole's villain Manfred, the central character of *The Castle of Otranto*, as 'laughable and powerless, not tragic'. How far, in your opinion, is her comment valid for this novel in particular, and for the gothic in general?

17 Imagine that as a film director you were given the brief of resurrecting a comparatively little known gothic classic for the cinema. Discuss the relative merits of Lewis's *The Monk* and Radcliffe's *The Italian* in this context before coming to a firm conclusion as to which would make the more effective film.

18 In what senses might it be more appropriate to consider Mary Shelley's *Frankenstein* as a philosophical, prophetic text than a horror novel?

19 Why do you think that, of all gothic fiction, it is Mary Shelley's *Frankenstein* and Bram Stoker's *Dracula* that have most vividly captured the popular imagination? Your answer should refer to texts and contexts.

20 'Jane Austen's novel *Northanger Abbey* in a sense validates the gothic as a serious literary force through paying it the compliment of parody.' Discuss ways in which parody – and *Northanger Abbey* in particular – serve to illuminate aspects of their subject.

21 Is it appropriate to see gothic landscape and gothic characterisation, in Heathcliff especially, as the driving forces in Emily Brontë's *Wuthering Heights*?

22 Roger Caillois has observed that 'The fantastic is always a break in the acknowledged order, an irruption of the inadmissable within the changeless everyday legality.' How helpful is this formulation for understanding Stevenson's *Dr Jekyll and Mr Hyde*? Might it apply also to other gothic texts?

23 Beckford's far-fetched early gothic novel *Vathek* contrasts strongly with the convincing, atmospheric realism of Susan Hill's *The Woman in Black*, and yet both may be termed gothic. Are there similarities, or only differences? Is the 'gothic' label of any use in this context?

24 Susan Hill maintains that 'I have never ever written anything which does not have a serious underlying purpose, or a moral of some sort, however oblique'. Does her tale *The Woman in Black* live up to her own words? Might they apply to other gothic fiction?

6 | Resources

Chronology of key texts and writers

1740s–1750s	'Graveyard' poetry, including Edward Young 'Night Thoughts' (1742), Robert Blair 'The Grave' (1743)
1757	Edmund Burke *A Philosophical Enquiry into the Sublime and The Beautiful*
1762	Jean Jacques Rousseau *Emile*
1764	Horace Walpole *The Castle of Otranto*
1781–1788	Rousseau *Confessions* (published posthumously)
1786	William Beckford *Vathek*
1789	William Blake 'Songs of Innocence', supplemented by 'Songs of Experience' (1794)
1791–1792	Thomas Paine *The Rights of Man*
1792	Mary Wollstonecraft *A Vindication of the Rights of Women*
1793	William Blake *The Marriage of Heaven and Hell*
1794	William Godwin *The Adventures of Caleb Williams*; Ann Radcliffe *The Mysteries of Udolpho*
1796	Matthew Lewis *The Monk*
1797	Ann Radcliffe *The Italian*
1798	Samuel Taylor Coleridge and William Wordsworth *Lyrical Ballads* (including 'The Rime of the Ancient Mariner')
1816	Samuel Taylor Coleridge 'Christabel' (unfinished)
1818	Jane Austen *Northanger Abbey* (posthumous publication, written 1798); Mary Shelley *Frankenstein* (initially anonymously)
1820	John Keats 'La Belle Dame sans Merci'
1840	Edgar Allan Poe *Tales of the Grotesque and Arabesque* (including 'The Black Cat')
1845	Poe 'The Raven'
1847	Emily Brontë *Wuthering Heights* (written 1845–1846)
1886	Robert Louis Stevenson *The Strange Case of Dr Jekyll and Mr Hyde*
1897	Bram Stoker *Dracula*
1898	Henry James 'The Turn of the Screw'
1919	Sigmund Freud 'The Uncanny' (essay)
1934	Dennis Wheatley *The Devil Rides Out*
1938	Daphne du Maurier *Rebecca*
1946–1959	Mervyn Peake *Gormenghast Trilogy*

THE GOTHIC TRADITION

1974	James Herbert *The Rats*; Stephen King *Carrie*
1983	Susan Hill *The Woman in Black*
1985	Clive Barker *The Books of Blood*
1991	Robin Jarvis *The Whitby Witches*

Further reading

Primary texts

Listed here are the key gothic texts referred to throughout this book. There are, of course, many others: this is a selection, intended to give a 'taste' of the gothic idiom.

Horace Walpole *The Castle of Otranto* (1764), William Beckford *Vathek* (1786) and Mary Shelley *Frankenstein* (1818) appear together in the 1968 Penguin edition (edited by Peter Fairclough with a useful introduction by Mario Praz

Jane Austen *Northanger Abbey*, 1818 (ed. Elizabeth Mahoney, Everyman, 1994)

C Baldick (ed.) *The Oxford Book of Gothic Tales* (Oxford University Press, 1992)

William Blake *Selected Works* (ed. David Stevens, Cambridge University Press, 1995)

Emily Brontë *Wuthering Heights*, 1847 (ed. Richard Hoyes, Cambridge University Press, 1997)

Edmund Burke *A Philosophical Enquiry into the Sublime and Beautiful*, 1757 (ed. David Womersley, Penguin 1998)

Angela Carter *The Magic Toyshop* (Virago, 1988)

Samuel Taylor Coleridge 'The Rime of the Ancient Mariner', 1798, illustrated by Gustav Doré, 1878 (Dover, 1970)

Peter Haining (ed.) *The Frankenstein Collection* (Artus Books, 1994) A fascinating anthology of relevant material, including other writing by Mary Shelley and film script selections.

Susan Hill *I'm the King of the Castle*, with an afterword by the author (Penguin, 1989)

Susan Hill *The Woman in Black*, with an introduction by the author and an essay on adapting the novel for the stage by Stephen Mallatratt (Longman, 1989)

Robin Jarvis *The Whitby Witches* (Macdonald Young Books, 1991)

Matthew Lewis *The Monk*, 1796 (ed. Howard Anderson, with an Introduction by Emma McEvoy, Oxford University Press, 1998)

Patrick McGrath and Bradford Morrow (eds.) *The Picador Book of the New Gothic* (Macmillan, 1991)
A collection of contemporary gothic fiction.

Iona and Peter Opie (eds.) *The Oxford Book of Narrative Verse* (Oxford University Press, 1989)
This includes 'Tam Lin' (anon), Coleridge's 'The Rime of the Ancient Mariner' (1798), and Edgar Allan Poe's 'The Raven' (1845)

Edgar Allan Poe *Tales of Mystery and Imagination*, 1839–1846 (with an Introduction by John Whitley, Wordsworth Classics, 1993)

Ann Radcliffe *The Italian*, 1797 (edited with an Introduction by Frederick Garber, Oxford University Press, 1981)

Mary Shelley *Frankenstein*, 1818 (ed. David Stevens, Cambridge University Press, 1998)

R.L. Stine *The R.L. Stine Collection: The Baby-sitter; The Boyfriend; The Girlfriend* (Scholastic Point Horror, 1993)

Robert Louis Stevenson *The Strange Case of Dr Jekyll and Mr Hyde*, 1886 (edited with an Introduction by Emma Letley, Oxford University Press, 1998)

Bram Stoker *Dracula*, 1897 (with an Introduction by David Rogers, Wordsworth Classics, 1993)

Edward Young *Night Thoughts*, illustrated by William Blake, 1797 (eds. Robert Essick and Jenijoy LaBelle, Dover, 1975)

Contextual and critical texts

Clive Bloom (ed.) *Gothic Horror: A Reader's Guide from Poe to King and Beyond* (Macmillan, 1998)
Pertinent and eclectic survey of 19th and 20th century comments on the gothic.

Fred Botting (ed.) *Frankenstein: Contemporary Critical Essays* (Macmillan New Casebooks series, 1995)
An authoritative collection, expertly introduced by Botting.

Fred Botting (ed.) *Gothic: The New Critical Idiom* (Routledge, 1996)
A readable, discursive and comprehensive account.

Kenneth Branagh *Mary Shelley's Frankenstein: The Classic Tale of Terror Reborn on Film* (Pan, 1994)
The film script, accompanied by contextual material, and lavishly illustrated.

Marilyn Butler *Romantics, Rebels and Reactionaries: English Literature and its Background*, 1760–1830 (Oxford University Press, 1981)
Includes plentiful references to the gothic and a useful Chronology.

Glennis Byron (ed.) *Dracula: Contemporary Critical Essays* (Macmillan New Casebooks series, 1999)
Another authoritative collection.

Richard Davenport-Hines *Gothic: Four Hundred Years of Excess, Horror, Evil and Ruin* (Fourth Estate, 1998)
Wide-ranging and eminently readable, appropriately illustrated study of various manifestations of the gothic.

Aidan Day *Romanticism: The New Critical Idiom* (Routledge, 1996)
A useful companion volume to *Gothic*, by Fred Botting, in the same series.

Boris Ford (ed.) *The Romantic Age in Britain* (Cambridge University Press, 1992)
Invaluable contextual information, clearly presented and covering the full range of artistic and cultural dimensions.

Lilian R. Furst (ed.) *European Romanticism: Self Definition* (Methuen, 1980)
As the subtitle suggests, an apt anthology of defining characteristics.

Marilyn Gaull *English Romanticism: The Human Context* (Norton, 1988)
Usefully and vividly setting the historical scene.

John Spencer Hill (ed.) *The Romantic Imagination: A Selection of Critical Essays* (Macmillan Casebooks series, 1977)
Another in this invaluable series on the critical approaches to literature.

Maggie Kilgour *The Rise of the Gothic Novel* (Routledge, 1995)
Approachable, original, perceptive study of gothic creations and criticism.

Raymond Lister *British Romantic Painting* (Cambridge University Press, 1989)
Contains excellent illustrations, including several distinctly gothic pictures, and a fine Introduction.

Raymond McNally and Radu Florescu *In Search of Dracula: The Enthralling History of Dracula and Vampires* (Robson, 1994)
Fascinating and exhaustively researched.

Katie Rodin (ed.) *In the Footsteps of Dracula* and Jim Pipe (ed.) *In the Footsteps of Frankenstein* (both Aladdin Books, 1995)
Colourful guides aimed at a young readership, but fascinating nevertheless.

Victor Sage (ed.) *The Gothick Novel: A Selection of Critical Essays* (Macmillan Casebooks series, 1990)
Probably the most pertinent yet in this series; an invaluable guide.

Muriel Spark *Mary Shelley* (Constable, 1988)
A well-crafted, fascinating biography.

Robert Woof, Stephen Hebron and Claire Tomalin *Hyenas in Petticoats: Mary Wollstonecraft and Mary Shelley* (The Wordsworth Trust, 1997)
The accompanying book to a biographical art exhibition, including interesting insights into Frankenstein.

Video and audio resources

Relevant videos include:

Frankenstein (1931) directed by James Whale, starring Boris Karloff; its sequel *The Bride of Frankenstein* (1935)

Frankenstein: The True Story (1973, TV version), directed by Jack Smight

Mary Shelley's Frankenstein (1994), directed by Kenneth Branagh

Dracula (1931, re-mastered 1999), directed by James Whale, starring Bela Lugosi

Bram Stoker's Dracula (1992), directed by Francis Ford Coppola

Dr Jekyll and Mr Hyde (1932), directed by Rouben Mamoulian

As Good as the Book (1998, Channel 4 Education TV series), with interesting programmes on film versions of *Frankenstein* and *Dr Jekyll and Mr Hyde*

Gothic (1987) directed by Ken Russell, and *Rowing with the Wind* (1988) directed by Gonzalo Suarez: both film accounts of the background to the writing of *Frankenstein*

ICT resources

Some of the more useful Internet websites on the gothic include:

The Varna Goths Literary Society, at
http://members.tripod.com/~intellectproductions/index.html

Romanticism on the Net (a broadly based site) at
http://users.ox.ac.uk/~scat0385/handbook.html

Goth is as Goth Does (a lively look at contemporary gothic themes) at
http://members.tripod.com/~BrokenLies/gothis.html

An academic forum for exchange of ideas, named Romantic Circles, at
http://www.newi.ac.uk/litweb/News.htm

An exhaustive list of further gothic sites through the Yahoo! Search engine, at
http://www.yahoo.co.uk/Society and Culture/Cultures and Groups/Goths

A fascinating site on gothic gardening, Something Wicked This Way Grows..., at
http://www.gothic.net/~malice

The Female Gothic, surveying the portrayal of women in gothic texts, at
http://www.engl.virginia.edu/~enec981/Group/ami.intro.html

Shelley's Frankenstein, focusing specifically on that central novel, at
http://www.georgetown.edu/irvinemj/english016/franken/franken.html

A Mary Shelley site, on her immediate social and biographical context, at
http://virtual.park.uga.edu/~232/mws.letandjour.html

More (extensive) insights into Romanticism and its relationship to the gothic, at
http://humanitas.ucsb.edu/shuttle/eng-rom.html#authors

Glossary of critical and historical terms

Circulating libraries developing during the 18th century, as literacy and book production grew more widespread, these institutions were essentially forerunners of the modern system of lending libraries. Membership was by subscription, thus limiting access to the fairly wealthy, but dissemination of books, including many gothic texts, was nevertheless wide-ranging. Circulating libraries frequently doubled as publishers and printing presses.

Closure the process by which a writer brings a text (particularly a work of fiction) to a definite conclusion.

Romanticism a tendency (or movement, according to some commentators) in thought and feeling which gathered momentum in the 18th and 19th centuries. A definition is elusive, but Romantics are likely to value individual, imaginative creativity founded on intensity of emotion, as against classical conceptions of orderly 'good taste'. Wordsworth's phrase 'the spontaneous overflow of powerful feelings' (from the Preface to the *Lyrical Ballads*, 1798) helps to give a flavour to the term.

The sublime a key term in the development of Romanticism and the gothic, the sublime is essentially concerned with feelings of spiritual awe and wonder, often occasioned by an emotional response to natural grandeur. Mountainous landscapes, for example, were seen increasingly as appropriate settings for sublimity of feeling. Although an ancient term, it was given new life in the 18th and 19th centuries – notably in Burke's *A Philosophical Enquiry into the Origin of Our Ideas of the Sublime and Beautiful* (1757).

Whig and Tory Parties loose groupings of British politicians which developed in the 18th and early 19th centuries as parliamentary politics assumed ever greater importance. The two names originated as terms of abuse that subsequently 'stuck', and were the precursors of the Liberal and Conservative Parties respectively. Whigs tended towards more radical policies than their Tory, largely land-owning, counterparts.

THE GOTHIC TRADITION

Index